PENGUIN BOOKS — GREAT FOOD

A Little Dinner Before the Play

From 1921 to 1922 AGNES JEKYLL (1860–1937), sister-in-law of Gertrude Jekyll, wrote a series of essays for the *Times* newspaper with titles such as 'Tray Food' and 'Sunday Supper'. A volume of these cookery columns was published as the *The Kitchen Essays* in 1922. A celebrated hostess, Lady Jekyll's first dinner party included among its guests Robert Browning, John Ruskin and Edward Burne-Jones. Full of insight, wit and comfort, *Kitchen Essays* champions the idea that cooking should always fit the occasion and temperament.

A Little Dinner Before the Play

AGNES JEKYLL

PENGUIN BOOKS

PENGUIN BOOKS

Published by the Penguin Group
Penguin Books Ltd, 80 Strand, London WC2R 0RL, England
Penguin Group (USA) Inc., 375 Hudson Street, New York, New York 10014, USA
Penguin Group (Canada), 90 Eglinton Avenue East, Suite 700, Toronto, Ontario,
Canada M4P 2Y3 (a division of Pearson Penguin Canada Inc.)
Penguin Ireland, 25 St Stephen's Green, Dublin 2, Ireland
(a division of Penguin Books Ltd)
Penguin Group (Australia), 250 Camberwell Road,
Camberwell, Victoria 3124, Australia
(a division of Pearson Australia Group Pty Ltd)
Penguin Books India Pvt Ltd, 11 Community Centre,
Panchsheel Park, New Delhi – 110 017, India
Penguin Group (NZ), 67 Apollo Drive, Rosedale, Auckland 0632, New Zealand
(a division of Pearson New Zealand Ltd)
Penguin Books (South Africa) (Pty) Ltd, 24 Sturdee Avenue,
Rosebank, Johannesburg 2196, South Africa

Penguin Books Ltd, Registered Offices: 80 Strand, London WC2R 0RL, England

www.penguin.com

The Kitchen Essays first published 1922
This extract published in Penguin Books 2011
This edition published for The Book People Ltd, 2011
Hall Wood Avenue, Haydock, St Helens, WA11 9UL

1

All rights reserved

Set in 10.75/13pt Berkeley Oldstyle Book
Typeset by Jouve (UK), Milton Keynes
Printed in Great Britain by Clays Ltd, St Ives plc

Cover design based on a pattern by Truda Carter from Poole Pottery's pattern books,
GC series, *c.* 1934. (Photograph copyright © Dorset History Centre.)
Picture research by Samantha Johnson.

ISBN 978-0-241-96071-4

www.greenpenguin.co.uk

MIX
Paper from
responsible sources
FSC™ C018179
www.fsc.org

Penguin Books is committed to a sustainable
future for our business, our readers and our
planet. This book is made from paper certified
by the Forest Stewardship Council.

Contents

Some Breakfast-Time Suggestions

Breakfast is the most difficult meal of the day, whether from its social or its culinary aspect. Many of us feel like that man who, meeting a bore, said, 'If you have got anything to say to me I wish you would kindly say it to somebody else.' Our reluctant consciousness, but newly returned from a dream world, shrinks from all but the gentlest contacts. 'Praise me not too much,' as Odysseus said to Diomed, 'neither find fault with me at all,' and the greetings of melancholic and dissatisfied individuals can, like the cry of the curlew in Miss Barlow's Irish idyll, set our whole mental landscape into a minor key for the rest of the day.

Not that we may permit ourselves too churlish a licence, as did that misanthrope asked by his talkative barber how he would wish his hair cut. 'In perfect silence,' came the discouraging reply! Fortunately there are some rare companionships which never come amiss, and their presence, even at the breakfast table, breeds perpetual benediction – some bright spirits who can irradiate the gloom of the most cheerless morning, even as 'the lark who meets the rain half-way and sings it down.'

A *cordonbleu* cannot be at her best very early in the day; and as for a chef, he will unblushingly delegate his duties to his understudy. It is wise, therefore, to aim at simplicity, but, within its limits, to strive after perfection. Above all

1

things, breakfast must be hot, and many breakfasters resemble Belconan the West Indian, who said of himself: 'No one sins with more repentance, or repents with less amendment, than do I.' That long metal food-warmer with spirit lamps known as 'the Sluggard's Delight', whereon porridge, coffee, and hot dishes can be kept palatable, is a great help. Insist on a hot-water kettle of real efficiency, on a tea-caddy which will contain a delicate as well as a pungent blend of tea, more than one tea-pot, and a small saucepan over a spirit lamp for boiling eggs, with an hourglass standing sentry near by. Readers of Jane Austen will remember Serle's unrivalled success in this minor art, and can emulate his skill. The French prefer eggs boiled in water rising from warm to boiling, instead of rushing them through by our rapid three minutes' process. But this claims, perhaps, overmuch attention from a busy hostess. Good coffee may come from Arabia or India, from the Blue Mountains of Jamaica, or *via* France with an admixture of chicory; but its flavour and excellence will be derived from daily careful roasting and grinding, a truism universally admitted and habitually disregarded. A fireproof jug of ample proportions with wide ventilated top should keep the milk hot without boiling over; and if you can persuade your kitchen to follow what used to be a universal practice in the northern coffee-drinking countries, the day will begin pleasantly for you.

FROTHED COFFEE.

Take 2 large tablespoonfuls of cream and froth it well with an egg-whisk, and pour it on the top of the hot milk just before serving. Each cup will get some of the foaming milk and both look and taste the nicer; and for a thin or specially deserving individual a spoonful can be surreptitiously skimmed off to cream a favoured cup. Having experienced this, you will not again sit down under the thick yellow blanket of scum which embarrasses all and disgusts many.

Toast, to be good, demands a glowing grate, a handy toasting-fork, and a patient watcher – counsels of perfection indeed, for the ideal rack is like friendship and the immortality of the soul, almost too good to be true. An anxious bride, humiliated by the sort of toast only a starving sparrow could relish, wrote to one learned in such matters, asking for a trustworthy recipe. 'Cut a slice of bread, hold it before the fire, and say incantations,' was the unhelpful but only advice vouchsafed. An electric griller can be used successfully by those who can successfully use such contraptions, but the elemental toasting-fork, the patient watcher before the fire, and a go-between, with the honour of the house at heart, are really the truest solution.

Here is a tried recipe for *Brioches*, very popular last summer on a big steam yacht, and worth the little trouble and practice required, especially for those of Continental breakfast habits.

Take ½ lb. flour, less than ½ lb. butter, 1 oz. sugar, pinch of salt, 3 eggs, ½ oz. baker's yeast. Weigh the flour and put one quarter of it in a basin with sufficient tepid milk to mix into a light dough. Put aside to rise for ten minutes. Put the rest of the flour into a basin, make a hole for sugar, eggs, and salt beaten together, and now mix in the butter lightly. When this sponge is ready, add to it the smaller quantity of flour with yeast, knead, and leave in a cool place. Next morning form into small cakes of cottage-loaf shape, the lower part as big round as a claret glass, the upper of sherry-glass size, and bake. This quantity will make twelve brioches.

Here is a popular *Marmalade*, that first necessity of the Englishman's breakfast-table, which so perplexed the French commissariat in 1914.

Cut 13 selected Seville oranges into thin slices, removing only the pips; pour 6 quarts of water on, and let it stand 24 hours. Empty all into the preserving pan and boil slowly for 2 hours. Add 10 lb. loaf sugar, and boil up again for 1 hour. Just before taking off add the juice of 2 lemons. If the preserve is required dark and thick, the rind of the oranges should be scraped before slicing them and added with the sugar.

Of Wedding Breakfasts

Marriage feasts resemble the institution they celebrate, of which Montaigne observed that those within its confines often struggled to get out, whilst those without endeavoured to get in. When the human contents of a spacious church are transferred into the few rooms of an average dwelling, the laws of the container and the contained are set at naught, and we shall agree with Arago that 'He is a rash man who pronounces the word "Impossible" anywhere, even within the sphere of pure mathematics.'

Those whose tribal instincts and gregarious tastes necessitate a long invitation list, may endeavour to reduce the ultimate crush (and not without success) by preliminary tea-parties and an evening reception; but a large proportion of guests will nevertheless attend on the wedding day, either because they enjoy the human drama, or fear lest their defection be counted unfriendly. Some few, of tried adoption, genuinely concerned in the fortunes of the adventurers, will wish to see the ship successfully launched on its uncharted voyage. Yet of all the actions of a man's life, his marriage least concerns other people, and it is ever the one most meddled with.

Wedding breakfasts in town are now generally reduced to the conventional stand-up buffet provided from outside, where choices of tea and coffee, hot or iced, of wine-cups and lemonades, of sandwiches and stuffed rolls, fancy cakes, ices, and some easily consumed sweet dishes are all that are expected, provided the appointments be dainty, the quality perfect, and the service dexterous. This recipe for *Iced Jelly* (for eight) may be suitable for any occasion when the guests are warm, the dishes cold.

Boil 2 calves' feet for several hours, strain off and leave to get cold. Remove all grease, and put them into a stewpan with the peel and juice of 4 lemons to each quart of liquor, ½ lb. loaf sugar, a piece of cinnamon stick and a few raisins, the whites of 4 eggs. Whisk all well together whilst boiling; strain through a jelly bag several times until clear. Flavour liberally with a sherry glass of maraschino, pour into an ice mould with secure lid, pack in ice and freezing salt in an ice pail, and freeze for 2 hours. Serve with a silver knife to cut it, and a bowl of fruit *macédoine*. The inner core should be firm and amber-coloured, the outside shell of a paler and more frozen consistency. Ordinary lemon jelly with sherry flavouring may be advantageously iced in the same way.

Biscuits Tuiles are a pleasant addition to ices or fruit: –

Take 3 oz. each of flour, white sugar, melted butter, 3 whites of eggs partly whipped, a little vanilla essence, 3 oz. chopped almonds. Mix together, place in small rounds on greased baking sheet, leaving room to spread. Bake golden brown, remove quickly on to a rolling-pin to dry and curl over.

Here also is a recipe for *Punche à la Romaine*, offered

in the hope that it may be of service for celebrating some marriage day or great festival occasion.

> Take 1½ pint orange and lemon syrup mixed, 1 pint champagne, ½ pint rum, ½ cup green tea, 4 whites of eggs whipped and stirred in gradually. It should be frozen soft, not hard, and served in wine glasses, either before, half-way through, or at the end of dinner.

The far-seeing parent will ensure a quick and tactful luncheon for the bride and bridegroom, in a room apart, with perhaps two or three favoured companions – some vitalizing consommé, a casserole of chicken with potatoes and peas, some dainty sweet or delicious fruit, and the drinks of their choice, would be suitable provision, and from this repast they must hasten to rejoin their guests and open the attack on that romantic survival, the wedding cake.

Country weddings must often take place early in the day, and so necessitate a more substantial sitting-down meal for everybody, small tables supplementing the large ceremonial one where are gathered the guests of honour. There the complicated foods we are so erroneously supposed to like, and so seldom do, are offered in bewildering variety; and mayonnaises, mousses, aspics, succeeded by elaborate creams, jellies, pastries, and ornamental cakes, appear in profusion, whilst confidential butlers pour champagne encouragingly into frugal glasses as the anxious moment for speeches draws near. Might it not be better to concentrate effort and expenditure on two or three really first-rate dishes of universal acceptance? Silvery salmon or sea trout, lobsters fresh from their rocky homes, peach-fed hams, abundant chickens hot, young, and undisguised, crisp lettuces, and perfect potatoes; compotes of fruit with generous bowls of whipped cream, cakes of the best, but not masquerading as flowers or towering into castellated buildings, all these would be welcome!

In both types of wedding breakfasts there is a tendency towards the conventional, the stereotyped, unworthy of this greatest day in life.

'Rarely comest thou, Spirit of Delight!' And what wonder, seeing the conditions of our welcome! If, instead of the refreshment caterer with his contract properties, Beauty's daughters were to prepare the feast, how lovely it might be and what a pleasure ground for memory! A table spread with white and gold brocade, a room hung with garlands of myrtle and bay, and generous sheaves of the perfect bridal flowers – roses, lilies and magnolias, tulips, carnations and orange blossom – all in their seasons. Great dishes and platters of silver and gold, or gleaming brass, piled high with fruits – peaches and grapes, pine-apples and plums, oranges, apples, melting pears – flagons of red wine, goblets of sparkling drink, delicious fragrance of rosemary, lavender, and cedar wood in all the air – unseen voices singing madrigals, music, laughter, and the love of friends. What an hour to remember later in the silence and the starlight.

We are a warm-hearted and sentimental people for all our so-called British phlegm, as was shown by the spontaneous rejoicing and sympathy evoked by a recent royal wedding, when a whole nation, as it seemed, were unseen well-wishers at the feast.

Even the most critical and cold-hearted must feel something of the dramatic solemnity of the rite and pass in silent review their own lives, so chequered with hopes, memories, and regrets. For always the Institution of Marriage can be, not only what the Prayer Book says it is, but also the means of enabling the happy and the fortunate to deal with many difficult matters, and to do many lovely charities for those less blessed than themselves, for the doing of which two heads and two hearts are – not better than – but the perfection of one.

Luncheon for a Motor Excursion in Winter

'In justice to the "Turk's Head", it should be clearly stated that it does no more to cow and discourage travellers than many other provincial hotels in England,' wrote a brilliant modern novelist lately; and a wit of the last century revenged himself for wrongs suffered, by the following impromptu written in a visitors' book at departure, and no doubt equally true to-day: –

'There stands an Inn below the hill, rightly named "Pelican" from its enormous bill.'

Similar experiences have suggested to many motorists of late that, until the innkeepers of 'this dear, dear realm of England' emulate their foreign competitors in the provision of desirable food at reasonable cost, a home-made picnic may often prove the more excellent way. Tough joints, bluish rabbit or pork pies, fly-haunted ham bones, black-eyed potatoes, cheese rocky as its birth-place in lovely Cheddar, musty biscuits, indifferent bread and butter, an atmosphere redolent of stale tobacco and beer, attendants haughty, sometimes hostile, generally indifferent until tipping-time approaches – these are not rare and isolated exceptions, but the daily fare of our long-suffering race when they take the road.

Let us, then, get out the luncheon-basket from amongst

the wedding presents of a richer age, and, in addition, contrive a small Norwegian kitchen or hay-box to hold a large screwed jar of comforting *Potage à la Écossaise* – meat, vegetables, and soup combined – a big thermos for *Mulled Claret*, and a smaller one for *Coffee*. Slip in a couple of camp-stools and a waterproof rug as well as our furs, so that we are not tied to the car or the road-side should some sheltered nook or sunny prospect allure us. Pour a moderately good bottle of claret into a saucepan, with half the rind of a lemon, 12 cloves, a pinch of nutmeg, a tablespoonful of sugar, and let these simmer, but not boil, serving very hot. Once experienced in perfection on a cold day it will not be forgotten, and should serve to warm and unstiffen the motorists without delay, whilst the luncheon is getting itself unpacked.

POTAGE À LA ÉCOSSAISE.

Put into rather more than a quart of good light stock some 2 tablespoonfuls of pearl barley (previously washed in cold water), a carrot, turnip, leek, onion, celery, a little cabbage or 3 or 4 Brussels sprouts, and let them cook gently together with the required number of nice cutlets from a well-selected and trimmed neck of mutton or lamb. Season with a little chopped parsley, cream, salt and pepper to taste, and a couple of teaspoonfuls of green peas, and some of those tiny new potatoes which the prudent housewife will have bottled like her goose-berries, or buried in a tin of dry sand for a winter luxury.

11

The 6½d. Bazaar again sells charming quite small square or round white metal tins and nice horn or wooden spoons for the appropriate consumption of this dish.

STUFFED SALMON ROLLS,
FOR SIX PERSONS.

First cook a slice of salmon (about ½ lb., and Norwegian might do), and when cold pass through a wire sieve and mix with a little mayonnaise sauce or whipped cream flavoured with a drop of Worcester sauce and tarragon vinegar. Add a pickled gherkin chopped small, and salt and pepper. Cut off the tops of the rolls or scones, remove the soft inside and butter them sparingly. Fill in with the prepared salmon, place a little shredded lettuce on top, and replace the lid with a thin slice of the buttered inside. A filling of egg and sardine, of minced chicken or game with cream and chopped walnut or beetroot, celery or gherkins, could be substituted, or some picked prawns or lobster with a little chopped aspic and salad.

For a *Winter Cake*, black and sticky with treacle, enlivened by whole white almonds, use this recipe: –

One pound of flour, 1 lb. black treacle, 1 dessertspoonful ground ginger, ½ lb. brown sugar, ½ lb. butter, ½ pint milk, ½ teaspoonful carbonate of soda, 4 eggs, a little finely-chopped citron, and white whole almonds for top. Mix the dry ingredients together, warm the milk and dissolve the butter in it, beat up the eggs, then add treacle and stir into the dry ingredients, beat well, bake ¾ hour. This mixture should be a running consistency before baking, so add more milk if necessary. Bake in a flat brick-shaped tin; or if preferred round and deep, a saucepan will serve.

Finally have a nice little selection for dessert instead of pudding, made up out of the following suggestions. A small cream cheese or Petit Suisse wrapped in a lettuce and some crisp plain biscuits with a tiny pot of red currant jelly (the combination so popular in Duval restaurants), a box of fresh dates or pulled figs, a carton of almonds and raisins, or a little screw bottle of large black French plums, or better still a basket of fresh fruit costing what your purse can buy or your fruit room produce, a handful of glacé ginger cubes or a tin of peppermint creams, and lastly the cup of hot coffee, black or white, tasting as good out of the thermos as tea tastes nasty. And though there is no fire there can yet be smoke of cigarette, cigar, or pipe, to taste.

Now comes the moment for a gentle 'promenade de digestion', or stretch across open country with a motor rendezvous at the end, for enjoying the scenery or local architecture, for taking intelligent interest in Roman camp or prehistoric remains, for noting the birds and sharing your food with them, for descending, like the prophet's ravens, with the surplus of your feast, on the nearest road-menders or country children, remembering to ask their acceptance thereof with all the courtesy you can command. Perhaps before you turn homewards you will collect a few delicate trails of ivy, better taken than left, from some wayside trees, to float in your flat bowl, or a bunch of late autumn foliage or winter ever-green to gladden your town home more intimately than florists' trophies. The nursery might be made happy by a sod of growing daisies from the hedgerow, such as have given great poets thoughts too deep for tears, and which could fill the empty luncheon receptacles, only forbearing to damage wild beauty which is everybody's possession. Such a day might well hold more material comfort and bodily invigoration, more imaginative sug-gestion as well as some saving to sorely-tried purses, than the hours often spent in stuffy public dining-rooms and crowded hotel lounges, for in the words of Meredith, 'when we let Romance go, we change the sky for a ceiling.'

Country Friends to a Christmas Shopping Luncheon

God made the first Christmas, and man has ever since been busy spoiling it. Year by year the propaganda of the shops grows increasingly active; and their suggestions for the keeping of that high feast, including such secular items as dozens of brandy, whisky, and champagne, appear annually more elaborate and incongruous than ever before. Experience leads us, however, to believe that their lavish wares will all be sold and bought, given and received, cherished or passed on, as in the long tale of bygone years. Country friends flock eagerly to town, armed with lists of the things they are resolute to buy and bestow, and the offer of a house of rest, an hour of respite from their bewildering preoccupations, and an agreeable luncheon will be an act of hospitality gratefully welcomed. It will be the more appreciated if we take the trouble to order such fare as is not readily procurable in the country, for the charm of novelty is a potent one. 'What is that delicious little cake?' her late Majesty Queen Victoria is said to have inquired with interest, on being confronted for the first time with a penny bun. For a first course, then, choose a dish of oysters, rarely procurable at their best either at the seaside or in the country, serving them in their own half shells 'au gratin', if not 'au naturel'.

OYSTERS AU GRATIN.

Choose the required number of plump native oysters, open, strain off the liquor, and beard them. Wash and dry the shells, butter their insides, shake over some fine stale bread-crumbs, and replace the oyster on a half shell. Cover it with more bread-crumbs, a little of its own liquor, a few grains of red or coralline pepper, a squeeze of lemon juice, and a very thin slice of fresh butter. Bake 10 minutes in a hot oven, and brown with a salamander. Serve hot with brown bread, butter, and a garnish of parsley.

For an alternative, try this *Malay Curry of Prawns*, which should recapture the true Eastern flavour for a Western palate.

One cucumber, 1 cocoanut, and allow 4 prawns a head. 1. Remove shells from prawns, putting them into a *bain-marie*, and covering with milk to simmer for the sauce, placing prawns aside till required. 2. Peel and cut the cucumber into pieces like a large olive, boil in salted water, strain off and drain when cooked, but not over-done. 3. Drain the milk from cocoanut, retaining for use at the last, grate a cupful of the white part, pour over some boiling water, and let infuse. 4. Put in a stewpan a piece of butter, adding when melted a small onion cut in fine rings to fry a golden brown. 5. Add a clove of garlic chopped very fine, a tablespoonful of *crème de riz*, a teaspoonful of turmeric powder, one of powdered cloves and cinnamon, a little salt, a teaspoonful of sugar; fry together, then add the strained liquor from the

prawn shells, the water from the grated cocoanut, cook
for a few minutes, then add the prawns and cucumber,
and let it remain as it is for ½ hour. 6. Slowly re-heat,
adding the milk from the cocoanut. 7. Serve in small
brown flat fireproof egg dishes with handles, encircled
by plain boiled rice which could alternatively be handed
separately.

Veal, so tough and dark in its country birthplace,
seems to become milk-white and tender in London,
where Jewish butchers or French speciality importers
produce it in perfection. 'There is many a man for whom
the devil lies in wait at the kidney end of a loin of veal,'
said a famous wit. So this might make a suitable dish to
follow, and should be carefully braised, a good stuffing
tactfully inserted, or added as a garnish in balls, together
with some curls of crisp bacon and midget sausages. A
moist purée of sorrel and well-browned potatoes would
be suitable for the accompanying vegetables.

A *Salad Course* as habitually given now at American
luncheon parties might furnish a pleasing variety from
established usage, and for the central dish a large green
bowl containing a mixture of green or sugar corn of the
largest shelled variety (as sold in tins by American
grocery importers), freshened and flavoured with a little
whipped cream, pepper, and red celery salt, and surrounded by pieces of white endive lubricated with oil
and vinegar. Or a fruit mixture might be preferred, such
as sliced banana, apple shavings, and white grapes,
mixed with some cream and set round with green hearts
of lettuce or curly endive moistened with salad oil and

lemon juice. With this serve very hot crisp biscuits, of the cracker variety or home-made water ones, and a fresh cream cheese; or try transparent slices of gruyère surrounding a heap of freshly-grated roquefort.

In Paris, *Gauffrettes*, or *Waffles*, are always a popular and inexpensive entremet, and the irons with which to make them are readily procurable there. Here waffles are more often seen in the Caledonian Market or in process of manufacture in the purlieus of the Adelphi than at the tables of the well-to-do, but if made according to the recipe below and speeded from fire to dining-table they should meet with the welcome they deserve. Ingredients: –

Two dessertspoonfuls of fine flour, mixed with 1 of white sugar distinctly flavoured with vanilla pod, adding 4 yolks of eggs and ¼ lb. butter creamed with a spoon. Whip the whites of the eggs separately and then whip these together, and incorporate them with the other ingredients. Have ready the heated and greased waffle tongs, and fill one side with the mixture. Close and cook on a bright heat till pale brown, serving on a warmed dish with vanilla flavoured powdered sugar snowed over. Butter the tongs between each waffle, which should take some 2 minutes each to cook. The accompaniment of a pretty glass jug or dainty bowl with cream lightly whipped, or a sauce-boat of hot golden syrup or maple sugar, would be welcome, but not indispensable.

A compote of fruit might, if liked, be provided as an alternative, and since delicious little yellow *Mirabelles* are rarely seen except in town they might be something of a novelty, and most big Stores produce them in tins or bottles.

After a fortifying cup of coffee, the shoppers will return with renewed zest to their afternoon campaign, and when a Christmas thank-offering subsequently arrives – as it may – receive it in the spirit of Theocritus, who wrote: 'Surely great grace goes with a little gift, and all the offerings of a friend are precious.'

Tea-Time and Some Cakes

Two divergent schools of thought contend round the tea table, the one belittling its importance, the other exaggerating its opportunities. They urge opposing points of view, often with an acerbity out of keeping with its temperate hospitality. Sydney Smith was moved to fervent piety as he poured out his third cup, 'thanking Heaven that he had not been born before the coming-in of tea'; and readers of Scott will remember in *St. Ronan's Well* the vehemence with which Meg Dods repelled Captain MacTurk's base insinuation: 'Me drunk, you scandalous blackguard!' she cried, waving her tempestuous broomstick, 'me that am fasting from all but sin and bohea.'

Of late the medical profession, reinforced by Fashion and Sport, both calling out for slimness and muscle in their respective votaries, has conspired against the sociable rite with its insidious accompaniments. 'What!' they say, shaking a forbidding finger in their costly confessionals, 'two cups of tea a day, my dear sir (or madam)! No wonder that you are ill!' 'Le fiv'-o'-clock' has in recent years established itself abroad, and we shall continue no doubt to enjoy its indulgences in spite of the slight sense of guilt which accompanies and possibly enhances their practice.

For the generation now passing away, tea was only clandestinely procurable by joining the children, and still it seems to have a special charm out of nursery mugs with hot toast made and buttered over the high fender as only Nurse knows how to do it, or shared on the schoolroom hearthrug surrounded by jam-eating clamorous youth, when it tastes so much better than on the gilt chairs accompanied by decorous drawing-room conversation.

During the war years even the office yielded to the allurements of afternoon tea, and the humours of its preparation by flappers, and its enjoyment by their principals, provided the caricaturist and the letter-writer to the papers with much happy inspiration and spiteful suggestion.

Hungry hunters and shooters, triumphant and bemired from the chase, love to quench their thirst and spoil their dinners under the stuffed heads in the great hall, and golfers and fishermen to magnify their exploits amid the miscellaneous companionship of the hotel lounge. All these confess the hour with grateful pleasure, but the true spiritual home of the tea-pot is surely in a softly-lighted room, between a deep armchair and a sofa cushioned with Asiatic charm, two cups only, and these of thinnest china, awaiting their fragrant infusion, whilst the clock points nearer to six than five, and a wood fire flickers sympathetically on the hearth.

George Herbert, in his poem beginning 'Content thee, greedie heart!' reminds us with superfluous cruelty that we cannot 'both eat our cake and have it', and though to try is as human as to fail, we should at least ascertain what our cake is made of and weigh carefully all its ingredients before deciding which we will do with it. Here is one called *Caraway Tea Bread* baked specially for the Nursery, which grown-ups will do well to visit on its afternoon début. Ingredients:

Three teacups of flour, 2 teaspoonfuls baking powder, 1 teacup castor sugar, 1 large dessertspoonful ground caraway seeds, 1 egg, 3 oz. butter, 1 teacupful of boiling milk. Mix flour, baking powder, and sugar, rub in butter, mix the milk warmed with the egg beaten and the ground caraway seeds. Knead into a flattish brick-shaped loaf or cake, and bake 20 minutes in a quick oven. To be eaten fresh, with a little butter.

For the hungry Schoolroom, when friends come to tea, here is an excellent *Stollen Cake*, and if treated more lavishly in the matter of candied peel and raisins, there is no board it might not suitably adorn.

One pound flour (½ lb. extra for kneading in), 5 oz. stoned raisins, 4 oz. currants, 4 oz. butter, 4 oz. sugar, 2 eggs, 2 oz. baker's yeast. Pour a little lukewarm milk over the yeast, mix the warmed flour with a little milk, add yeast, and mix. Place the dough in a warm place to rise for an hour. Mix in the melted butter, eggs, sugar, fruit, grated peel of a lemon, and some candied peel, and knead well with remaining flour. Put back to rise for 1 hour. Place the dough on a baking sheet, making it into an oval flat shape, fold one side half over, brush with egg, strew with halved almonds and sugar. Bake 45 minutes in a hot oven. Sprinkle with icing sugar when baked.

Here is something for the dyspeptic guest who never eats anything at tea, followed by something for the robuster one who occasionally eats too much.

BROWN FLOUR BISCUITS.

Half a pound brown flour, 6 oz. butter, a pinch of baking powder, another of salt. Rub together, mix with milk, roll out thin, cut in wine-glass-sized rounds. Bake 5 minutes in a hot oven.

For a festive occasion try this: –

SUPER-CHOCOLATE CAKE.

Half a pound fresh butter beaten to a cream, 7 eggs (yolks and whites beaten separately, and the whites stirred in the last thing), ½ lb. best vanilla chocolate grated and heated in oven, then beaten up in the butter with 3 oz. dried flour, ½ lb. sifted sugar, 4 oz. ground almonds, 1 teaspoonful of sal volatile. Bake in a slack oven, then ice with thin soft icing flavoured with maraschino. If ingredients are thoroughly beaten up it will be very light.

Lest this last calls for a reproach from the thrifty, here is a nice useful cake suited to the Rector's 5 o'clock call, or the ladies of the local political organization in conclave, and good for the office luncheon tin or the fisherman's basket next day.

WARDLEY CAKE.

Half a pound ground rice, ½ lb. flour, ½ lb. butter, ½ lb. castor sugar, ½ lb. crystallized or glacé ginger, a few glacé cherries, ½ pint milk, ½ teaspoonful bicarbonate of soda. Warm the butter and milk, and add them to dry ingredients, mixing well. Bake at once for from 2½ to 3 hours.

As a final suggestion, here is a sand-cake for a syren's tea-party of two. It was known in the Vienna of happier days as a *Venus Torte*, and might be served with honey-dew and the milk of Paradise when procurable.

Clarify 1 lb. butter. When cold beat to a cream, add 12 oz. sugar, 1 lb. potato flour (sieved), 4 whole eggs and the yolks of two, the zest of 1 lemon. Beat the whole mass for 1 hour, when it should form bubbles. Bake in a buttered and finely bread-crumbed mould in a moderate oven. Halve these quantities for a small cake.

A Little Dinner Before the Play

One of the compensations of an annual return to the city after summer holidays and to the more serious life of the winter months is to be found in the wealth of good things offered for our improvement and relaxation as the long evenings close in. In the words of Mr. Kipling:–

> Bar home the door of summer nights
> Lest those high planets drown
> The memory of near delights
> In all the longed-for town.

One of these near delights is assuredly a good play in congenial company after a pleasant dinner. This, to be successful, must be planned with care, and neither timed so late as to produce hurry and consequent irritation, nor so early as to disconcert the busy and encourage the unpunctual. The table must not be served with too many good things, lest they induce lethargy, nor yet must the tired worker arise hungry and unrefreshed. A course of *Soup and Fish combined*, one satisfying meat or game dish, with vegetables and salad, another merging sweet and dessert into one – this will be more acceptable to eager play-goers as well as more considerate to any elders of sensitive digestion and leisurely habit than the customary more protracted meal, and should admit of perfect and unruffled service.

SOUCHET OF SLIPS.

Allow one slip for each person, skin and trim off sides and head, put the trimmings into enough good stock for number required, add some vegetables, and let simmer gently for 2 or 3 hours. Strain and clarify in the usual way for consommé. Prepare a julienne of carrots, turnips, and leeks. Add these when cooked to the cleared soup, and simmer altogether for half an hour or so, the slips meanwhile to be placed in a fireproof dish and poached in salted water. When ready to serve, boil up soup, pour into a hot tureen, adding the slips drained from their water, and serve together in soup plates, with horse-radish-cream sauce, and brown bread and butter going round at once with it.

CÔTELETTES EN ROBES DE CHAMBRE.

Take selected lamb or mutton cutlets. Grill them lightly and leave to get cold. Take some good gravy stock and mix in a little tomato purée. Add fine cut ham or tongue, or both. Spread some of this thickened sauce on to each cutlet, and wrap them round with a jacket of lightly-made puff-pastry. Cook them in a brisk oven till nicely browned, and serve very hot on a long, narrow dish, accompanied by the same sauce, only less thick, in a sauce-boat and by a pile of French beans, or peas, 'à la crème', sharing another long dish with a *Purée of Mashed Potatoes*, not that stiff and tasteless compound so often offered, but the French variety made by boiling and draining the potatoes, and then mashing them in a saucepan lightly rubbed with a clove of garlic, and mixed with a liberal amount of butter, and either boiling milk, or, as some cooks prefer, with a little stock from the soup-pot, which makes it a little browner; and this need be hardly thicker than a well-made apple sauce. Another method would be to boil a Portuguese onion very soft, and beat it hot with four times its weight in potatoes, adding cream, butter, pepper, the yolks of 2 eggs, and salt, and pass through a sieve. Make this mixture into round golf balls, and flavour with salt, pepper, and chopped parsley, brush with egg and fine stale crumbs, and brown in the oven on a buttered tin, and serve on the same dish as the green vegetables.

If lighter nourishment be preferred, a fat *Quail* cooked and served inside a puff-pastry jacket, the legs just peeping out, should emerge moist but done to a turn, and accompanied by a salad of blanched endive surrounding a sparely sweetened compote of Russian cranberry. Or, as an alternative suggestion, choose *Bécassines Flambées* (Snipe on Fire), a bird to each guest, to appear on a silver or metal dish, perfectly roasted, and sitting each on a toast lightly fried and spread with the liver, etc., well pounded. Outside the serving door let a couple of tablespoonfuls of brandy, previously warmed in a small casserole over a spirit lamp, be set alight and poured flaming over and around the birds just as they come to the table. Crisp potato straws or thin fried rounds of Jerusalem artichoke and a salad of celery shredded and enriched by cream, and surrounded with watercress or lamb's lettuce, should accompany this dish.

To combine the sweet and dessert courses into one, a fruit dish seems desirable, and a nice looking *Pine-apple* with a decorative top might be chosen, the upper end sliced off so as to give an adequate opening by which to scoop out the fruit and juice and make of them a delicious cream or water ice as preferred, in the approved manner, and this can be served inside the pine-apple standing upright, its top being replaced for its first introduction to the party. With this, send round an ample shallow cake covered with soft icing, well flavoured with maraschino and decorated with glacé cherries or some preserved cubes of pine-apple cut in half. If liked, the cake might have a layer of soft icing inside as well. An alternative suggestion, if ice is not desired or pine-apples are too expensive that day, might be to choose some large seedless juicy oranges, one for each guest, removing the top and with it an inch or more of the fruit, which must be all scooped out, cut and shredded small, and returned to the lower and larger half of the orange, minus pith or pip, and plus a syrup of the juice enriched with curaçoa or sherry. A thin méringue mixture, replacing their own top halves, and lightly coloured in a quick oven, then left to cool, will bonnet them attractively, and a short sojourn in the ice-box give them a refreshing chill. With these might come in a flat sponge, or similar cake, flavoured with orange-flower water, and roofed over with a soft icing – this also orange-flavoured with rasped rind, and decorated with candied orange rings cut up.

There should still be time for a perfect cup of coffee

and a possible liqueur, and, most desired of all by many, for a good *smoke*, without which there will be no social fire. Warmed thus and fed, the play-goers will be attuned to enjoyment and ready to appreciate each other, their dinner, their play, and their hostess, 'and so to bed with great contentment.'

A Little Supper After the Play

There is a sharp cleavage of opinion between the pleasure-seekers who prefer a reinforced tea or a stirrup-cup of soup and a sandwich before an evening's entertainment, with prospect of supper to come, and those who will have the accustomed meal at 6, 7, or 8, and 'won't wait.' The hour when the play begins, the claims of the working day, and the locality of the home are the deciding factors. The restaurant has its drawbacks, and those are fortunate who can command, especially in winter, a pleasant meal by their own firesides, with no anxiety in the matter of procurable drinks, no waiting for disengaged tables, no apprehension as to adequate ready money for that unknown quantity, the bill, that embarrassing problem, the tips. Few households can cope with the preparation of a hot meal late at night, except as a very occasional dissipation, but with one servant in attendance there should be no difficulty in arranging for a good supper with a marmite of soup kept hot on a metal food warmer or spirit lamp. This recipe is a comforting one, and suitable for a chilly night: –

CONSOMMÉ À LA INDIENNE,
FOR SIX PERSONS.

Put into a stewpan a quart of good stock, slice into it 2 onions, 1 large cooking apple, a tablespoonful of desiccated cocoanut, a dessertspoonful of curry powder (or more if it is liked hot), and the carcass of a roast chicken, rabbit or game bones, and let simmer gently for an hour. Strain and remove the fat, and clarify in the usual manner. Re-boil and serve with pieces of game or chicken in the marmite, and a very little plain boiled rice, also kept hot, to be added into each portion as helped.

A long dish of oysters is universally popular with men, but the oysters must have first-class references and be freshly opened, and served very cold, with brown bread and butter, red pepper, lemon quarters, white vinegar handy. Women often find it more blessed to give than to receive their proportion of 4 to the male 6, and these are perhaps easier to have very good at a first-rate restaurant or oyster bar than at home late in the evening. A good alternative is a cold *Soufflé of Lobster*, prepared and served up just before the cook goes to bed. This recipe is excellent also for summer luncheon parties, or as an extra course at dinner.

Choose a lobster weighing a little over 1 lb. for six or eight guests. Take all the fish from the shell, saving fair slices of the best parts for decorating the top; chop the remainder very fine, and mix with ¼ pint whipped cream, and season to taste. Pound the shell well, and add a little butter, and simmer on the fire with about 2 tablespoonfuls of milk. Strain through muslin, and add when cold to the cream and lobster. Melt about 4 leaves of gelatine and stir into the lobster cream. Have ready a round white china or silver soufflé dish with crisp shredded lettuce, hard-boiled egg, bits of skinned tomato, a little thin mayonnaise sauce passed through it all, reaching half-way up the dish, and put above this foundation the mixture of lobster; and when set put over a thin layer of aspic jelly slightly pink with cochineal and the selected pieces of lobster, and serve very cold with bread and butter.

For the *pièce de résistance* try a *Chaud-froid de Volaille*, made with the best parts of 2 chickens, or 2 pheasants, or a small turkey. These should be cut up, after boiling, into fillets or neat helpings, and when cold enriched with a spreading from a tin of purée de foie gras, or the remains of a terrine; and if there are any truffle peelings available so much the better. Lay these fillets on a long silver or metal dish, mask them thinly with liquid aspic, with more finely-chopped aspic at the ends as a garnish. Between each fillet arrange upstanding sheaves of uncooked celery, finely cut and encouraged to curl so that it looks in shape like a shock of corn ready to be carried, and is white with cream well whipped and seasoned with salt and pepper and a drop of tarragon vinegar. Any other cold salad garnish of single lettuce leaves or small skinned tomatoes could embellish this dish.

THE *ASPIC JELLY*

to be made with a pint of brown stock, adding a little carrot, onion, celery, parsley, and a few pimentoes (allspice), with a dessertspoonful of tarragon vinegar and a teaspoonful of Worcester sauce. About 8 leaves of gelatine and 2 whites of eggs whisked all together in a stewpan. Place on stove and bring slowly to the boil. When clear, strain through a fine cloth into a basin and use as required.

For sweets nothing is nicer than this specially good *Orange Jelly*. Not that stiffly moulded, colourless, and acid variety so usually and deservedly rejected, but soft and shapeless, of the colour of a blood orange, and really tasting of the fruit, served in a large shallow glass dish, and accompanied by another dish containing a fresh *Compote of Oranges* made in the approved way, the fruit uncooked, all pith and pip removed, and a hot syrup of sugar and juice poured over the orange segments and allowed to cool.

RECIPE FOR OLD-FASHIONED
ORANGE JELLY.

Half a pound loaf sugar, 18 oranges, 2 lemons, 1 oz. gelatine. Boil the sugar to a syrup, pour it boiling hot on the thinly peeled rinds of 2 oranges. Squeeze the juice of all the oranges, pass through a silk sieve, add the dissolved gelatine and syrup and a few drops of cochineal, and serve in glass bowl not moulded. With this jelly and fruit have a plate of thin long *Caramel Biscuits* which are generally purchased at a costly confectioner's, but are not difficult to accomplish at home, given one in the kitchen who can make good pastry.

Make some light puff pastry and roll it out in castor sugar instead of flour, and cut it into long narrow shapes, some 6 to 8 inches long, and 2 to 3 inches wide. Bake in a medium oven very brown and crisp and blistered, and rather sticky, like brandy snaps.

As regards supper drinks, it rests with the host whether champagne or sparkling moselle, white wine, whisky and soda, or temperance drinks such as orangeade or dry ginger-ale and cider mixed, be provided. The male oyster-eater would welcome a glass of porter with that course, whilst feminine taste would go in the direction of Chablis. Some good cigars and cigarettes, a bottle of liqueur, and some sweets should not be forgotten, and will promote the success of the evening.

Of course the prudent and far-seeing would eat and drink none of these things: they would partake of a cup of hot Benger by their own bedsides. But, then, these suggestions need never have been written, and the evening would assuredly have ended but tamely – 'Eudaemonia (Happiness) is a good daemon,' said the Ancients, and a wise poet of our own day (John Masefield) bids us –

> Best trust the happy moments – what they gave
> Makes man less fearful of the certain grave,
> And gives his work compassion and new eyes –
> The days that make us happy make us wise.

P.S. – Don't forget some hot bovril and sandwiches for any motor-men waiting to take the guests home; you will thereby be doing as you would be done by, and the supper-party will be the merrier and more prolonged.

Dance and Supper

The New Year has always begun socially with festivities, but surely the practice of dancing has never been so universal and continuous as in the present time. The homes of England, as well as the provincial town halls and newer village institutes, have of late years followed the example of the London restaurants and dance clubs, echoing nightly, and often from tea-time onwards, to the strains of orchestra or jazz band, of pianola or gramophone. Even the churches are showing their widened sympathies by the promotion of dancing and cards within their folds. The admonitions of two widely dissevered counsellors of youth would in these days have been wholly superfluous. 'Sacrifice to the graces!' reiterated Plato to his disciples: 'Delay not to take the best dancing-master you can hear of,' wrote Lord Chesterfield to his son. And could they but revisit the glimpses of the moon, would not they too be enslaved by the prevailing passion, which, dominating old and young alike, has transformed the thoughts and habits of busy and serious persons to a surprising extent. The chaperon also is forging her way slowly back to an almost obsolete bench, whence she, too, can join the dance. Eating and drinking – as always where people congregate in numbers – have become a matter of acute interest and urgent effort. 'The oldest and youngest are at work with the strongest,' wrote the

observant Wordsworth; 'there are forty feeding like one!'
Where space is a consideration, it may be well to organ-
ize refreshments continuously throughout the evening,
thus avoiding the special crush inseparable from a defin-
ite supper hour with its disappointments and delay; and
the musicians, adequately fortified early and late, would
only then require brief interludes for refreshment and no
prolonged supper interval. Round tables seating eight to
twelve, supplemented by quite small ones tucked in
where possible, are always more popular than a stand-up
buffet; and if tea, coffee, lemonade, and ices can be dis-
pensed from a separate tea-room, it lightens the strain on
the supper-tables. Here is a recipe for some nice biscuits
and for orangeade, the speciality of a famous Parisian
restaurateur, for the tea-room.

CINNAMON BISCUITS.

Three oz. butter, 3 oz. castor sugar, 6 oz. flour, 1 egg,
1 teaspoonful powdered cinnamon. Beat butter and
sugar to a cream. Mix cinnamon with flour, adding it gradually; moisten this mixture with beaten egg till a stiff
paste. Roll out, and cut into cakes with a round cutter;
sprinkle with chopped almonds. Put on a baking sheet
in a moderate oven.

ORANGEADE.

For every 3 quart glass cup-jug, take the rinds of 2 lemons
and 2 oranges, peeled very thin; place these in *bain-marie*
with 1 dessertspoonful of white sugar to each orange, and

bring to boiling-point. Cut 6 oranges and 2 lemons in halves, squeeze and strain their juices into a thick white kitchen jug; add the syrup made from the rinds, etc., and put on ice. Just before serving in glass cup-jug, add an iced syphon of soda, or 3 small bottles of soda, or soda added to plain water, as preferred. Use blood oranges when procurable, otherwise colour with a drop or two of cochineal and float 2 or 3 slices of the fresh fruit. Always serve very cold.

On the supper-room tables may be assembled all the most attractive things that can be devised for easy consumption (preferably with fork and spoon) under the alert supervision of one detailed to refresh and replace food and drink before the changing guests. Soup of the clear consommé type should be available early and late, and there is generally a special run on it when the party breaks up: twenty quarts for a hundred guests and twenty-four quarts of lemonade or orangeade would be an approximate provision. A large but delicately made *Quenelle* of cream of chicken or veal, moulded the size of a dessert spoon, with a few peas or vegetables reduced almost to a glaze, placed in the centre of the quenelle, and covered in with a little more of the chicken cream, and poached lightly in water, kept hot, and one slipped into each portion of the consommé when served, gives distinction to the soup. Or *Clear Tomato Soup* with a spot of whipped cream on a tiny croustade, or *Consommé à la Indienne*, made with chicken carcasses and lightly flavoured with grated cocoanut, curry paste, and a few grains of rice, would be a little out of the common run.

Sandwiches can show infinite variety, and the popular kinds are too well known to require description, but here are two sorts, perhaps rather less obvious: –

ŒUFS À LA CRÊME.

Cut round slices, wine-glass size, from French roll or bread, boil the eggs hard, pass through a sieve, season with pepper and salt. Then whip some cream and stir in the eggs lightly, spread thickly on the buttered bread, add a soupçon of chopped lettuce or cress, and lay the twin buttered slice very lightly over it.

The same rounds *à la Guyon*, spread with shrimp or salmon paste, a slice of peeled tomato cut the long way of the fruit, and made into an oblong sandwich with a sprinkle of chopped cress, are good.

For a good cold *Cream of Chicken* for the supper table, steam a large plump fowl till tender. When cold pound the meat, and pass through a hair sieve mixed with enough cream to make it light, season to taste, add 3 or 4 leaves of gelatine dissolved. When nearly set, pour it into a plain round charlotte or brick-shaped mould previously lined with aspic of the chicken stock, turn out, and serve very cold with a garnish of shredded and creamed celery, or a fruit salad, or chopped aspic and cress. A similar treatment of lobster makes a good *mousse*, and the economist can use whiting for its basis. Both these can also be served in small individual mould shapes, if preferred, round a centre of salad.

Large *Silver Bowls of Macédoine*, made with Bartlett

pears quartered, Cape plums halved, peeled, and stoned, and some fresh pine-apple with plenty of claret-coloured syrup is a safe stand-by. As also are glass bowls of *Tangerine Jelly*, each made with 12 tangerines, 1 quart water, 1 oz. gelatine, and from 6 to 8 oz. sugar, treated as for lemon jelly, with sections of skinned and pipped tangerine showing through the jelly, and a little sprinkling of finely-shredded skin; a small glass of curaçoa or yellow chartreuse improves it.

A boiled turkey, robed in white béchamel, spotted with black truffle peelings and attended by a sugar-cured ham, can shelter on the serving table till required. Its presence gives confidence to the anxious hostess, and wholesome food to the wise and prudent. When champagne is absent, this cider cup, as served at a restaurant of world-wide reputation, may possibly be preferred to wine: –

For a 3 quart glass jug of *Cider Cup*, place 2 quart bottles of cider and 2 bottles of soda-water, or a syphon, on ice for 2 or 3 hours according to season. Just before serving, put in a jug 2 oz. castor sugar, a liqueur glass of brandy, a wine glass of sherry, ½ wine glass curaçoa, and a wine glass of *sirop de grenadine*. Pour in the cider and soda water, float pieces of whatever fruit you may have – apples, oranges, pine-apple, strawberries, peach, cherries – with a slice or two of cucumber, and a lump of ice. A liberal dash of orange juice is a great improvement.

Their First Dinner-Party

The first dinner-party is always an interesting event in a newly-founded home, and should be so organized as not to monopolize the attention of host and hostess to the exclusion of social enjoyment. It must not err on the side of parsimony, nor yet by its lavishness vex those new relations or old aunts whose attitude has been aptly characterized as 'affectionate, but hostile'. 'Not fewer in number than the Graces, nor yet exceeding the Muses,' runs an old adage regarding the perfect party; so, avoiding both danger points, let the table be well and truly laid for eight cheerful guests. All beginnings are important. If you can establish a name for having good food by a series of successful hospitalities, friends will grow lyrical over your cold mutton, and even ask for the recipe of the Shepherd's Pie – so potent and mysterious are the workings of suggestion! On that principle oysters or caviare might well be ordered to head the first menu, but they are costly additions, and, as George Meredith was wont to say, 'Economy, our dread old friend, must decide!'

Clear soup gives the cook her first chance, and already a dress rehearsal will have given a taste of its quality. Having attained to a well-flavoured consommé, cut some carrots, onions, celery, turnips, into very small dice, if for a *Brunoise;* and into fine strips with the green parts of leeks added, if for *Julienne*. Cook these slowly to a golden colour in plenty of butter for an hour (the butter does again for similar purposes), and sprinkle them lightly with white sugar. Drain them dry, put them into the simmering consommé, and let them gently cook for from 1½ to 2 hours. Skim off any grease before serving.

The fish course must be chosen with reference to the market and the special aptitude of the cook. *Filets de Soles à la Creme, Pommes Pailles*, is safe, choosing medium soles, one to every four guests, the fillets nicely trimmed and put into a buttered ovenproof dish with seasoning, and covered with buttered paper.

Cook for 10 minutes and fold together, dishing with some of their own liquor mixed with some heated cream poured over them, on a long hot metal dish, potato straws of the length and thickness of the smallest wax match, well dried before immersion in very hot lard and drained dry afterwards, heaped at either end, and sprinkled along the edges. A sauce boat with a good mousseline sauce could be added, and in that case the fillets should be served less moist.

For the *pièce de résistance* a very small *Selle de Pré Sâle* (Saddle of Welsh Mutton) in winter; in spring a tiny saddle of English lamb would be hard to beat. That any reproach of dullness may be taken away, treat it thus: –

For a saddle weighing about 8 lb. take some 6 lb. of turnips; when cooked squeeze through a cloth to get out all the water; mix with a little stiff white sauce or thick cream, add pepper and salt, make very hot, carve the saddle into long thin slices as required for number of guests, fill the space so cleared on either side with the purée of creamed turnip, replace the slices crosswise above it, pour over a little very hot gravy. The kidneys, taken out before roasting the saddle, and cut into rounds, fried with their fat left on, can be served on or about the saddle, or sharing a long dish with new or purée potatoes, together with the other vegetables chosen, and followed by a bowl of red currant jelly or mint sauce. A nicely-prepared vegetable course might be interpolated after the roast; peas *à la Française*, or asparagus with hollandaise sauce, would be the most popular selection.

For a sweet, choose *Crêmes Glacées Tutti Frutti*, taking for eight persons: –

One pint of cream; add 1 dessertspoonful each of cura-çoa, maraschino, and rum. Whip until light; serve in small glasses, preferably like the small size of Pyrex round glasses, wider at the top than the bottom; allow sufficient cream for each portion, and freeze in the ice cave for 1½ hour. Before serving, lay round the edges a gay but narrow ruching of finely-cut crystallized fruits, an apricot, greengage, pink pear, red cherries, all shred-ded, mixed, and saturated with the same liqueurs; tea-spoons on the dish between each glass and small fresh home-made macaroon biscuits to accompany.

A ripe camembert, with hot oat-cakes, crisp water biscuits, and well-iced butter may be preferred to a savoury; for dessert one dish of the most beautiful fruits in season mingled in picturesque variety; choose also carefully those sweets men often affect to disdain but more frequently enjoy. The wines, cigars, coffee, and liqueurs must all be as good as you can afford, and the *Barley Water* – for many guests like an alternative drink – should be cold and plentiful, but restrained as to sugar and lemon juice.

Here is a recipe often greeted as perfect; but barley water can, like coffee, a spring day, and a charming woman, produce miracles of variety out of the same constituents: –

Wash three tablespoonfuls of pearl barley in a quart of water two or three times changed and thrown away. Put a fresh quart of water with the barley, bring to the boil, simmer slowly for 10 minutes. Strain into a jug, add juice of 2 lemons, sugar to taste, and set on ice till wanted. Enough for three or four.

Having given of your best, inevitable criticism must be borne with philosophy, remembering the motto inscribed on the walls of a certain ancient Scottish college: 'They say – What say they? – Let them say!'

Sunday Supper

Sunday hospitality is a problem which, in these days of diminished service and increased social activity, cannot be solved without forethought and tact. The kitchen and the pantry both claim and deserve consideration and some liberty; but against this, relations and friends can often meet only at the week-ends, and drift hopelessly out of touch unless some point of contact is made pleasurable and easy. The lonely or hardworking bachelor, too, male or female (for the term has come to include both sexes), is specially grateful for Sunday welcome, and inspiration for the future as well as sympathy in past and present interests are oftenest sought and found on 'the day which comes between a Saturday and Monday'. Sometimes a group of relations or friends can evolve a system of mutual hospitality; but all inelastic bands are apt to snap disagreeably, and any feeling of obligation is ruinous to spontaneous companionship. Of late the restaurant has often had to solve the difficulty; but, except for a *tête-à-tête*, this can hardly be considered a general solution, if purse, health, or privacy are to count. Rather let adequate provision, made beforehand, liberate as many workers as possible, and the well-furnished side-tables, where each can supply individual needs with little or no service, give a sense of freedom and informality which will compensate for any slight diminution of comfort. If the number of guests be known and limited, a cold meat course might be attractively presented for each one in some such fashion as this: Purchase or cut thin slices, circular as the base of the dinner plates, off a rolled and spiced round of beef, or long slices off a brick of cold pressed beef; ally with it a slice of tongue or ham, and pour over both a thin sheet of well-flavoured aspic jelly – some attractive bits of lettuce or watercress and a gay radish or two, cut into rosy-edged slices and imprisoned in the jelly. This will make an inviting supper. Alternatively, some pieces of white boiled chicken in béchamel on a *mousse* made of their own less delicate parts not wholly devoid perhaps of some purée of foie gras, with pale aspic chopped small, and green beans, peas, or quarters of tomato as a garnish; or, best of all, with the half of an American pickled peach and some salad. If pickled peaches are considered extravagant – as, alas! they are – a good substitute can be made with the best quality of evaporated apricots, well steeped and softened in clove-flavoured water and treated with a little vinegar or lemon and a few drops of brandy or liqueur. These are good also as fruit salad with any cold meats. Cold ducks stuffed with a delicate *mousse*, cold chickens stuffed with rice made savoury with tomato or pimentoes, or an uncut leg of lamb set round with little jelly castles of mint sauce made with aspic and chopped mint – these, together with a bowl of appetizing potato salad, will deprive the visitor's bell of half its terrors, and the impetuous hospitalities of irresponsible youth might then pass uncensured.

POTATO SALAD.

Take kidney or the most waxy potatoes obtainable, boil in their skins, peel while warm, cut into thickish slices, pour on 1 tablespoonful vinegar and about 2 tablespoonfuls stock, but very gradually so that they may absorb it; add 2 tablespoonfuls oil, some pepper and salt to taste, and 1 small finely-chopped onion, and let it all stand for an hour before serving. A very, very thin mayonnaise sauce with a little French mustard and a drop or two of garlic vinegar, and a few capers with parsley and chives may be used as an alternative dressing.

This cold *Mousse of Whiting and Lobster* (for six) is a nice supper or warm weather luncheon dish.

Boil 2 good-sized whitings, and when cold pass through a fine wire sieve with a little cold salmon, and put it into a basin with salt, pepper, cream, and half a teacup of liquid aspic jelly; thoroughly mix. Line a brick-shaped or charlotte mould with aspic; when set put in a layer of lobster cut in small pieces, then half fill with the fish *mousse*, then another layer of lobster, and fill up the mould with the rest of the fish; pour over a layer of aspic, and leave to set. Turn out, and serve with a cucumber, beetroot, or other salad, with green sandwiches of brown bread and butter and a bowl of mayonnaise sauce.

Attractive sweets are always easy to make or procure, and the simpler ones – such as *macédoines* of fruit with a Devonshire junket or creamy rice, or méringues, or a bowl of orange jelly, or trifles – are hard to beat, but a *Chocolate Marrée* or an *Open French Tart* might have for some the glamour of a new acquaintance which could ripen into friendship. For the first, take ¼ lb. of the best chocolate *à la vanille* you can find or afford. Let it steam over a stewpan of boiling water for 30 minutes; then gradually work into it 4 raw yolks of eggs till smooth; whisk the whites to a stiff froth, and mix all together lightly. Pour into a shallow round glass dish, and let it stand 12 hours, and serve cold and white with 6d. of fresh cream poured all over it, and these *Vanilla Crescents* in attendance. Take 2 oz. each of sifted sugar, fresh butter, ground almonds, pastry flour, and a pinch of baking powder, a little salt, a bit of vanilla pod scraped. Mix all into paste; make some cords 5 to 6 inches long and thick as a middle finger, and shape them into flattish horseshoes. Cover with white sugar, and bake in a moderately hot oven for 20 minutes.

FOR THE FLAT *TART*:

Line the bottom of a round fireproof or oven glass dish with good short pastry; bake a golden brown. When cold spread with a liberal layer of lemon cheese mixture; on the top of this a layer of home-made raspberry jam, and cover all with some slightly-whipped cream.

But at Sunday supper it often matters less what is on the table than what is on the chairs; and if these are fortunately furnished, preceding suggestions could be disregarded, and 'a loaf of bread, a jug of wine', might be found entirely adequate provision.

Tray Food

Ill-health may be said to resemble greatness in that some are born to it, some achieve it, and some have it thrust upon them. The number of those who, for one cause or another must perforce dwell apart, eating the bread of exile, is no inconsiderable one, and in the interests of the invalids – temporary or permanent – of the disabled, of the baby's mother, of the rest-cure cases, of those in quarantine after or before infectious disease, of those recovering from surgical operations, it may be useful to consider how meals, of vital importance to their comfort and restoration to health, may be made more acceptable than they often are. Most of us have suffered during temporary disablement from exasperating trays, all the most important items – salt, pepper, mustard, sugar, bread, milk – omitted, their glass and crockery appointments so ragged and ill-assorted that no nourishment could appear attractive in their company, and the food itself chosen and presented without one touch of the capacity for taking pains which we are told is of the family of genius, and which can outweigh mere culinary skill or lavish expenditure on delicacies.

More attention to the technique of tray meals, then, is undoubtedly called for, and every house should possess attractive trays in various sizes and japanned in cheerful colours, leaf green, lemon yellow, sunset red, sea blue.

Though light in weight they must be capacious, having 'a parapidge for safety' and being easily allied to the necessary bed table. Also, they should have allotted tray-cloths and napkins in gay and harmonizing effects, their china, glass, and other accessories daintily matched or contrasted. The hot-water plate and cover, companion of those long-drawn-out meals of our nursery days, can be retrieved and furbished up; lustre ware both of silver and gold give a touch of brightness to the tea or break-fast sets; fireproof jugs and dishes of green, brown, or blue, and oven glass in small pie-dish shapes, or round with *cloche* covers for eggs and fish *au gratin*, or mush-rooms, vegetables, or cooked fruit, will ensure heat, which is a primary necessity. Of late, jugs constructed on thermos principles, and commonly used in America for iced water, are on sale in our first-rate china and glass shops, and these adequately preserve the extremes of heat and cold for an unpunctual sick-room, surely a great consideration where sleep often counts more than nourishment. Small food-warming trays, with jugs and toast racks, over a tiny spirit lamp will easily keep toast and coffee hot should its arrival be untimely or its con-sumption delayed.

Remember that the whole tone of the day can be set into a happy major key instead of into a mournful minor one by the mere aspect of the breakfast tray. A cheerful cherry – glacé or fresh – will render irresistible the skilfully-prepared and iced grape fruit on a hot day; a seedless orange halved and treated in the same way, beautified by green leaves of its own, or the nearest resembling foliage (and even villa gardens can boast a laurustinus bush); a gay pottery saucer of thin slices of banana with brown sugar and cream, a slice of melon, a tiny bunch of grapes, summer fruits in their seasons, and the health-giving apple accompanied by its ingenious little plated corer and wooden platter – all these may render nourishment welcome. A bunch of violets or primroses, a single rose, a sprig of heather, a spray of lemon verbena would bring a reminder of fresh life and loveliness from the outdoor world. To those bored with tea, coffee, and cocoa, even at their best, the unexpected and clean wholesomeness of well-made *Cocoa Nibs* might be welcome.

Take 2 quarts cold water to a teacupful of unbruised cocoa nibs, and let simmer without boiling in an open saucepan till reduced by half. Add 1 pint cold water and boil till reduced to half the quantity; add a second pint, and again reduce by boiling; finally add a third pint of cold water, and simmer till reduced to half. Never put on the lid during the process, which will take from 5 to 6 hours. If properly made it is a beautiful claret colour and free from all bitterness, and should be served with hot milk, cream, and a little coffee sugar.

For the mid-day meal serve as the principal 'plat' a nicely cut and fried bread *canapé* some six inches by four inches and one inch thick, and on to this spread a thick layer of well-made purée of chestnut with a couple of stoned and heated black plums at each corner. On this lay several delicately-cut slices of pheasant or turkey roasted or braised, and a little good gravy poured very hot over it. Or if chicken be the order of the day, make a bed of savoury rice on your *canapé*, enriching it with sultanas steeped in hot white wine or stock, and mixed with almonds split and grilled brown, and pieces of the breast laid on it. Again, slices of goose or duck reposing on a mattress of thick apple sauce above the *canapé*, or partridge breasts resting on softly-mashed potatoes and some mushrooms buttered, grilled, and added piping hot. Even the familiar slice of roast mutton from the family joint would acquire additional merit if supplemented by a creamy layer of mashed turnips, and a nice little pile of capers or a soubise sauce to add zest. All these might appear as off-shoots from the family dinner.

To vary the pudding course, make this *Cutchi*, or savoury custard, good hot or cold, in small round oven glass or white china individual ramekin cases, and send with it gossamer slices of brown bread toasted brittle in a slow oven.

Milk ½ pint, 3 whole eggs, 2 oz. freshly grated parmesan cheese, a little mixed mustard, nepaul pepper, and salt to taste. Beat well, and steam ½ hour, the water boiling when you put the little cases into the stewpan, but not after.

Tea-time, the invalid's happiest moment, might produce these little *Quaker Oat Pyramids* which can boast the four modern cardinal virtues of novelty, niceness, wholesomeness, and economy: –

Quaker Oats ½ lb., butter 6 oz., castor sugar 5 oz., 8 drops essence of almonds. Oil the butter, mix the oats and sugar together. Form a well, into which pour the butter and essence. Mix lightly into heaped tablespoon-fuls on a specially well-greased baking sheet, and put into a very slow oven for about ¾ hour. Do not remove from baking sheet till cold, else they crumble. The cakes should rise in little pyramids some 3 inches high from a base round as a claret glass rim. Half this quantity will make ten cakes, but as they don't keep well, let nurse or nursery enjoy the surplus.

On Savouries

Some people abstain from sweets at certain seasons, on grounds of religion or health, but seek compensation for their self-denial in tasty savouries; others never eat sweets because they dislike them, but expect something to replace them; and by many a dinner which does not include both sweet and savoury is thought, even in these days of shortened meals, to be a little disappointing. A few suggestions, then, as to savouries may not come amiss, though in France, that spiritual home of the great artists in cookery, a savoury course intervening between a sweet and dessert is looked on as something barbarous, indeed almost immoral. Morality, however, as Samuel Butler reminds us in his often startling notebooks, 'is the custom of one's country, and the current feeling of one's peers; so that cannibalism is quite moral in a cannibal country.'

Our lusty forefathers liked their savouries hot and strong, and *Toasted Cheese*, redolent of mustard and beer, bubbled its way down the long tables, a red-hot iron glowing within its pewter serving-dish. Nowadays, fireproof china or the chafing-dish solve the question of service, and there should be no excuse for its not hissing into the dining-room, with a forerunner of freshly-made hot toast. There are many good recipes, but this is a favourite for a savoury dear to those who have dined lightly and can slumber deep. For six people, allow about 6 oz. of a good toasting cheese, single Gloucester or mature cheddar; shred it finely, and mix it with a breakfastcupful of good white sauce, made with milk, butter, and a very little flour in the usual way. Stir this over the fire till the cheese is melted and smoothly incorporated, let it boil, pour it into a heated white china oblong fireproof eared dish, and serve whilst still bubbling and seething together with mustard and hot toast. Toasted cheese is apt to be stringy and tough if undiluted.

A nice savoury of *Oysters au Gratin* can be made by serving two or three hot on a scallop shell with their own moisture, and a tiny grilled roll of bacon above some buttered bread-crumbs, a squeeze of lemon, and a taste of cayenne completing the preparation before a lightning transit from fire to table.

Marrow Bones with hot toast and lots of pepper, though ogre's food, are too good not to be sometimes invited to the party; but let them appear rarely, and in the absence of the sensitive.

These *Croûtes de Laitance* make an excellent savoury.

Serve the hot soft herring-roes moistened with milk or butter on long thin narrow strips of well-made and nicely-browned puff pastry, about 6 inches by 2 inches; if the herring-roes are small, allow two, overlapping, to each person; a light dusting of coralline pepper is an improvement. This also makes a nice first course luncheon dish.

A hot toast spread with some anchovy-flavoured butter or paste and covered with several roes, and the white of an egg stiffly whisked and flung on it for a moment before it leaves the fire, is a homely savoury for a cosy dinner of two.

Little puff-pastry boats made in small moulds sold for the purpose came into fashion for dinner-party savouries recently, and can be filled with all manner of cargo, such as eggs scrambled with cheese, or cold, hard-boiled, and chopped with a little gherkin and capers; sardines made into a purée beneath a thin veil of soufflé mixture, or of savoury custard, slightly browned in the oven; anchovies beaten with cream into a cold cayenne flavoured *mousse*, coming chilled from the refrigerator with a thin sprinkle of cress; but beware of over-elaboration.

The least complicated savouries are often the best, and caviare or slices of foie gras, ice-cold with hot toast, or hot truffles *en serviette* with ice-cold butter, or thin slices of smoked salmon with brown and white bread and butter are the gourmet's choice, although few fortunes or consciences are sufficiently robust in these days for luxuries so costly.

A novel and successful savoury was evolved the other day thus, and called *Croûtes aux Prunes Farcies*.

Make nice little *canapés* of fried bread, about 2 inches by 3 inches, 1 for each person; take the biggest French plum procurable (or 2), soak it and extract the stone; fill the cavity with a stuffing of Scotch dried haddock, cooked, flaked, and beaten with a little cream and red pepper to a smooth *mousse*; serve hot.

Mushrooms are useful for savouries, but great care must be exercised in their selection, and any stale or doubtful ones rejected. American cuisine has invented special Pyrex glass saucers with bell glasses fitting over them, in which mushrooms are cooked very simply with salt, pepper, cream, and butter, so as to retain their juices and fugitive flavour; but this might be thought too profuse a savoury for the end of a varied dinner, when these little *Croûtes de Champignons* would be considered daintier.

Make a purée by frying about ½ lb. mushrooms, or steaming them, in some butter. When cooked, pass through a wire sieve, mix with a little stiff béchamel sauce, salt, and pepper, heap this on some fried or toasted croutons of bread, and on the top of each little mound place a small whole grilled mushroom and serve very hot.

Unsweetened wafer biscuits with grated cheese flaked liberally on to them and served very hot from the grill, also hot thin water biscuits spread with a savoury dressing of grated cheese and mustard, with flavouring of Worcester or Harvey sauce, and sent round with a cold cream cheese and celery or cress, will be counted amongst the best preludes to a good glass of wine. Perhaps it is as well that we live in our desires rather than in our achievements, and if the ideal savoury has still to be discovered, many ambitious cooks can use their brains and skill in its elusive pursuit

Meatless Meals

A certain *maigre* luncheon on a sunny Friday of an early summer, now far away and long ago, was vividly impressed on the mind of one of the party of four who enjoyed it, partly because of the beauty of its setting and the stimulating interest of the talk in that brief hour of refection, but also because of the discovery that such very simple things could be so much better than the elaborate and expensive ones which often complicate the sweet uses of hospitality. The garden room of an educational institution set amongst those lovely wooded hills which dip to the sea near Dublin, a Jesuit father of great intellectual distinction and goodness, a nun with a 'divine plain face', and two searchers after truth – this the scene and the party. Never before had newly-laid eggs scrambled so deliciously with young asparagus, or pink-fleshed trout tasted so fresh in the company of tiny potatoes and crisp lettuce. A wholemeal loaf and milk scones were there, with home-made cream cheese; the first fruits of the bee-hive also, tasting of the scent of lime trees in blossom, and the last fruits of the dairy in golden butter. Woodland strawberries, harbingers of the summer, in leaf-lined baskets, gave out their fugitive aroma, and finally a brown jug of coffee freshly roasted and ground, hot and fragrant beyond all previous experience, brought its valedictory blessing to a perfect meal.

How gross in comparison appeared the joints of butcher's meat, the slaughtered game and poultry of daily life, until the great reconciler, custom, should blunt afresh our susceptibilities! Since meatless days are the rule of many at certain Church seasons, and of many more at all seasons, some suggestions for making *maigre* menus more generally acceptable to all may not come amiss; for did not Mary Coleridge remind us in a pleasant volume of table talk that 'Self-sacrifice is the noblest thing in the world, but to sacrifice other people, even for a noble thing, is as wrong as persecution.'

Here is a breakfast or high-tea notion for a busy worker on a long winter's day, when time and thoughts race too quickly for more deliberate nourishment: A crumpet with lots of butter and salt; on it an egg, or maybe two, perfectly fried, the pepper-mill just going out of action, and all served piping hot in a warmed muffin dish. This is moderate in cost, simple in preparation, nourishing, and nice.

Here are two soups of proved excellence – one for coast dwellers or those near a good fish-market, and owning a well-filled purse; the other for everyman and everywhere. For a restrained and anglicized *Bouillabaisse* for four –

Make about a quart of fish stock in the usual way, with the trimmings, bones, and shell of the fish and lobster to be used subsequently. Cut up 2 large onions, and fry them in ½ gill of Lucca oil, add a teaspoonful of flour, a tumbler of white wine, pepper, salt, a fagot of parsley, a bay leaf, and 3 tablespoonfuls of tomato sauce. Boil from 15 to 20 minutes, pass through sieve, and return to saucepan. Cut up a small lobster into pieces, also a gurnet, bream, or flounder, of which the trimmings have been already utilized, for the fish stock. Boil ½ hour on a quick fire with the prepared stock, put a slice of bread, or preferably several small slices from a French roll, into a warmed tureen, transfer the fish with a strainer on to the bread, pour the broth over all, and serve together. When time is a consideration, as before some evening performance, this portmanteau of two courses is useful.

EVERYMAN SOUP, FOR FOUR PERSONS.

Melt in a stewpan 1½ oz. butter, stir into it smoothly 2 tablespoonfuls *crème de riz* flour. Add 1 quart milk (or if permissible, some light veal stock and milk mixed); let it cook for 10 minutes. Then add 2 tablespoonfuls freshly-grated parmesan or other cheese, and some pieces of macaroni previously washed and boiled in milk and cut into ¼-inch sections; or get some of those small shell-shaped Italian pastes called *coquilli* procurable fresh in Soho. Just before serving, pour the boiling soup on to a yolk of egg mixed with a little cream; stir all smooth, and pour into a hot marmite pot.

Clever *maigre* combinations of eggs, fish, vegetables, and fruit give abundant scope for culinary talent. Try for a useful luncheon dish: –

ŒUFS MOLLETS. SAUCE FROMAGE.

Boil your finest eggs soft inside, firm when peeled and skinned; balance them on circlets of fried bread within a low rampart of dry boiled rice; send them round with a bowl of bubbling hot cheese sauce made by stirring into a pint of nicest thin béchamel a ¼ lb. grated cheddar; to be ladled out over the eggs and rice.

If your cook has the puff-pastry touch, a *Vol-au-Vent* case confers distinction on all manner of noble relics, united in the bonds of a good sauce. Sea-kale boiled tender in milk and cut into short lengths, and diluted with béchamel, varieties of haricot beans, mildly curried and mixed with cauliflower, remains of fish with lobster or shrimp sauce, and, best of all, creamed oysters, will compose suitable fillings if skilfully treated.

THATCHED HOUSE PUDDING.

This old country-house favourite is really too nice for Lenten fare, but it could give opportunities for self-denial, and might come in usefully at any season. It is worth rehearsing into perfection if the first attempt should prove a little uncertain. Melt 2 oz. butter, add 4 tablespoonfuls flour. Pour in enough boiling milk to the consistence of a hasty pudding; add yolks of 4 eggs and grated rind of 1 lemon, with a little juice and sugar to taste. Whisk the whites stiffly, and add to the mixture. Put all in an oven-proof dish (a Pyrex glass one, 10½ inches by 6½ inches by 2 inches, just holds this quantity for six or seven).

Cook from 15 to 20 minutes. Before serving and after it has risen, pour over the top a cupful of hot thin apricot jam, and sprinkle with a liberal ounce of browned and chopped almonds.

With so many good things for meatless menus to choose from, our thoughts need never turn to what we lack, but rather find contentment in all we have.

For Men Only

Old prejudices die hard, and even before the days of Martha, cumbered with her much serving, the kitchen was looked on as specially the woman's sphere of influence. Yet those who have been privileged to stay in bachelor households or to dine at restaurants with their men friends, will often admit their superlative capability both in running the domestic machinery with noiseless and well-oiled efficiency and in ordering a better dinner from a chef or maitre d'hôtel than most women would be able to achieve.

What female intelligence can decipher rapidly those hieroglyphic sheets when presented in restaurants and unerringly select the 'spécialité de la maison,' or the most acceptable 'plat du Jour'? She will vacillate between the super-strange and the ultra-commonplace, or, losing her head, will select the cheapest of the mysteries proffered, or else plunge recklessly for something expensive and out of season. Sydney Smith boasted of his custom of stopping his female servant when encountered in the passage and asking her suddenly 'whether she preferred duck or chicken?' in order that she might acquire the good habit of swiftly making up her mind. Perhaps the old nursery game of Oranges and Lemons may conceal some such educative value, but choosing well is one of the most difficult things in a difficult world, seeing how profoundly it may affect our whole moral and physical well-being, whether applied to food, drink, companionships, or occupations, and that always our 'Choice is brief and yet endless.' Some people will never learn to choose, but, like the child at the birthday party asked what it would like to have, say, 'A little of everything, please.' That way madness lies.

Nor, gentlemen, is your efficiency confined to the ordering of meals; it is shown also in your rapid diagnosis of a difficult situation, in your successful handling of individual psychology. A domestic crisis involving the immediate disappearance of the entire kitchen staff from a remote country house, filled to overflowing with three cheerful generations of holiday makers was narrowly averted one August by prompt and successful male action. Shortage of water, absence of coal, conflicting milk claims between rival nurseries, momentary loss of temper on the part of the principals, and disaster seemed imminent and irretrievable. 'But what did you say to them all?' asked a trembling and defeated mistress when he returned cheerfully from the back regions. 'If you are a sensible woman, and I think you are, you will never ask or try to find out,' was the enigmatical reply. But, anyhow, the barometer was set fair, and the dinner that night specially successful. Was it flattery? Was it largesse? Was it that combination of a square jaw and a twinkling eye which is often so persuasive? No one will ever know, but the kitchen was a place of sunshine after storm, and the cook even volunteered to write out for one appreciative guest these recipes for her best efforts; so whatever the guilty secret, it was surely a case of justification by works, and only a man could have so handled the situation. Do not let September pass without trying each one of these dishes, all well suited to the season.

CLEAR TOMATO SOUP.

Cut in slices 1 lb. fresh tomatoes, and put into enough ordinary clear soup for, say, six people; simmer gently for 1 hour, strain through a clean cloth, re-boil, and serve with fried croutons, about two-shilling-piece size, piled with stiffly whipped cream, one to each person on a separate plate. The cream softens the acidity of the tomatoes and greatly improves the flavour.

PERDRIX AUX CHOUX.

Take 2 partridges and prepare in usual way. Old birds can be utilized in this recipe if necessary. Braise them carefully with plenty of vegetables and stock for 1½ hour. Take a red cabbage, shred it finely, and put in boiling water for 5 minutes. Strain, and put in a casserole with a breakfast cup of good stock, a dessertspoonful of French vinegar, an onion, some fat bacon cut in small pieces, a dessertspoonful of castor sugar. Stir well, and stew or braise for an hour. Take out the onion, and heap at either end of a long hot dish with the birds in the centre. For more than four people increase the quantities.

SYSTON ICED PUDDING.

Cut a sponge cake, the size of the mould to be used for pudding, in slices – a brick shape about 8 inches by 4 inches is good. Soak the cake with brandy and sherry. Prepare some stiffly whipped cream, sweetened and flavoured with brandy, and lay it in the mould alternately with dried glacé and brandied cherries between each layer of cake. Fill the mould full, cover in with buttered paper, and freeze 3 hours. Make a purée of apricots, with jam or bottled fruit, add brandy or sherry, or a little curaçao flavouring, put in the ice box to become very cold, and pour round the pudding.

CAMEMBERT IN ASPIC.

To 1 pint brown stock add a little carrot, onion, celery, parsley, and a few pimentoes (allspice), 1 dessertspoonful of tarragon vinegar, 1 teaspoonful of Worcester sauce, about 8 leaves of gelatine, and 2 whites of eggs. Whisk all together in a stewpan, place on stove, bring slowly to the boil. When clear strain through a fine cloth into a basin. Remove the paper covering from a ripe camembert and slightly scrape it. Select a round tin a little larger than the cheese and pour in the liquid aspic to 1 inch in depth; let it set. Then place the cheese in the tin, pouring in sufficient liquid aspic to cover it; leave it to set. Turn out when ready, garnish with watercress sprigs, and serve with thin oven-dried crisp toast. Cream cheese can be treated thus, and ice is not a necessity, only in hot weather it takes longer to set the aspic without it.

Bachelors Entertaining

Let us picture a bachelor living in a modest London house or in country surroundings near to his work, with a married couple, or oftener a working housekeeper, to look after him. Being constantly entertained by his friends and relations, he naturally desires occasionally to offer something in return. Problems of hospitality for such are oftenest solved by inviting their friends to a restaurant dinner or play – an agreeable but expensive solution – or by invitation cards for luncheons or teas at some race meeting or popular cricket match, when all responsibility is taken over by the club or contractor. This sort of entertaining, however, welcome as it may often be, seems to lack the personal note, for we do not really know our friends until we can visualize them in their own surroundings, and take interest in the gathered treasures or the pursuits of their homes. A host, moreover, feels and appears at a greater advantage by his own fireside than in the garish setting of a public restaurant, and might well say with Touchstone: 'When I was at home, I was in a better place!' Time often handicaps the host who has succumbed to the temptation of admitting the disturbing presence of woman into his sacred seclusion, for he may find it irksome to consider dinner problems whilst bacon and eggs are yet in his mouth, and the morning train relentlessly approaches.

Possibly, then, a few suggestions of simple but not too obvious dishes may not come amiss, and should be more generally useful than a single detailed menu, for purses and tastes, seasons and cooking facilities, differ widely. Moreover, any of these dishes can be exchanged or supplemented for popular and easily obtainable things such as bottled turtle, or tinned tomato soups, with caviare and foie gras or more homely *hors d'œuvres* to precede them. If the fish market be near, oysters, lobster, or dressed crab might be summoned, or the help of the cooked provision merchant invoked for dressed meats and pies, for ham, tongue, or galantine, and the recently developed pastry-cook artist might delight and surprise with his wonderful creations in cream tarts and decorated cakes. But there is surely a want of individuality about entertainments built exclusively on preserved and ready dressed provisions, and the dictum of an eminent Victorian housekeeper still holds: 'Give your friends what you have yourselves; only have enough of it, and make it a little nicer.'

Stychy Polonaise is an easy and comforting soup, the speciality of a gay little half-underground restaurant in distant Warsaw.

> Cut in square-shaped pieces some carrots, turnips, leeks, celery, cabbage, according to quantity required. Fry these in butter with a pinch of salt and sugar, add some good brown stock sufficient for expected guests, and let all simmer gently for about an hour; remove any grease. Thicken with a dessertspoonful of brown flour liquefied with stock, boil up, and add a little cream before serving.

Cod and Oysters au Gratin, sufficient for four persons, would be a good selection for winter.

Steam about 1½ lb. of middle of cod; when nearly cooked remove skin and bone, break into pieces, make a good creamy white sauce, put the fish into a greased fireproof dish with six or more oysters bearded and cut in half and pour over the sauce. Next sprinkle over liberally some browned buttered bread-crumbs, a little freshly-grated cheese, a restrained dusting of mild red pepper, and a squeeze of lemon juice. Place the dish in the oven to get very hot. A few pieces of boiled cod's liver dotted here and there may be added with advantage. This makes an excellent winter luncheon dish, and with a little practice a plain cook can accomplish it to perfection.

Boiled Mutton is a dish reminiscent of the seaside boarding-house table, but no less a connoisseur than King Edward VII. was especially fond of this transfiguring version of it.

Boil the best end of a neck of tender mutton (four to six cutlets), dip in oiled butter, roll in coarse white dried bread-crumbs, and grill for some 15 minutes. Serve in a large oven-proof dish surrounded by small piles of nicely-prepared vegetables, such as new potatoes finished in butter and chopped parsley, with some small glazed onions, and sprouts, carrots, beans, turnips, peas or chopped sprue braised in a little stock and butter, all nicely cut and disposed around. Send with it a clear gravy in a sauce-bowl with plenty of capers and finely-chopped pickled gherkin, and in addition sprinkle both of these last items sparingly over the grilled meat.

Savoury Puddings can be made with a chicken jointed and cut up, some ½ lb. sausages cut into biggish pieces, and some veal collops; or alternatively with game such as plovers or black game, grouse or partridge, past their first youth. They require the addition of thin slices of tender steak rolled up small or enwrapping the boned joints of game varied by slices of cooked ham, and perhaps a kidney or two cut up with small mushrooms is an improvement. Good gravy made from the livers and carcass bones of the birds, with seasoning of herbs, chopped parsley, salt, and pepper are necessary, but given good material no sauce or wine should be required. Interline a buttered pudding basin with a light suet paste, chop a little meat small for furnishing the ground floor, so to speak, add the other ingredients, and cover over with paste. Boil very slowly, for some 2 hours or more, serving in the same basin neatly dressed up in a clean napkin.

Caramel of Oranges and Cream is a nice and recently evolved sweet.

Make a salad of thick slices of orange, carefully excluding pips, pith, and skin, and lay in a glass dish or pretty bowl. Make a thin syrup with the escaped juice and white sugar, adding a little extra juice if required, and pour on this. Take ¼ lb. loaf sugar, and stir in enamelled or copper pan with ½ tumbler of water over the fire till melted, and then let it boil into a not too dark caramel, taking some 10 minutes. Pour this out to get cold and stiffen; crush it coarsely when hard and crisp, and shake it over the fruit. Cover all with some well-whipped cream – ¼ pint will suffice – and on to this sprinkle a few almonds, browned and roughly chopped.

For a savoury, make or buy some small round very thin water biscuits. Spread these when cold with a mixture made of a tablespoonful of fresh butter, a dash of Worcester sauce, and a teaspoonful of either chutney or a thick hot sauce such as *Diable*, all worked into a thin paste. Put the biscuits into a quick oven for some five minutes. Serve very hot, with a very cold fresh cream cheese, and some curls of celery or radishes.

There are pauses of service in the best regulated dining-rooms, when solace is sought in crumbling or nibbling something. Salted almonds are expensive, and by many thought indigestible; they can be understudied by a packet of the American cereal *Puffed Wheat*. A few spoonfuls of this, crisped hot in the oven and lying invitingly on small mother-o'-pearl shells, or in some such decorative and labour-saving receptacles before each guest, will comfort the shy, stem the torrent of the fluent-obvious, and generally promote a flow of that pleasant conversation, such as the late Lord Acton yearned for when he bade his friend remember that 'One touch of *ill* nature makes the whole world kin.'

For the Too Thin

Many women of the present day are below their proper weight in relation to their age and height. With some this is the result of what our fashionable American friends call 'Starving for Shape'; others object to eating many of the ordinary foods on grounds of principle or humanitarianism, so that, without pressing for specially cooked dishes (an egotism many shrink from), they frequently go without adequate nourishment. Both sexes often restrain their natural appetite for athletic reasons, wanting to ride, run, and dance light, and to excel in games and sports where weight is a handicap. Numbers of influenza convalescents, too, get reduced by illness, and their doctors will urge them 'to feed up', 'to put on weight', knowing by experience how excessive thinness induces nervous disorders with resultant neurasthenia.

The fattening properties of milk, farinaceous puddings, and sweets with Devonshire cream, of plenty of fresh butter with bread and potatoes, and of oatmeal, pulses, and cereals, of root vegetables and some fruits – these are too well known to require stressing. But inclination often fails, and fashion cries 'Beware'. A few attractive dishes are therefore suggested, hoping to make the observance of doctor's orders something of a pleasure as well as a duty, their niceness being, as it were, the smile on the face of the stern lawgiver.

SARDINES À LA SACKVILLE.

Make a nice purée of potato a little moister than the ordinary mashed preparation; place a thin layer, when cold, on an oblong silver or china dish; cover this with a layer of sardines, boned and skinned; mask this over with a thin coating of whipped cream; place on this a further layer of mashed potato, more sardines, and cover over with the remainder of your shillingsworth of cream, whipped, peppered, and salted; finish with a sprinkle of coralline red pepper and a few sprigs of surrounding watercress. With it send round Veda brown bread and butter. For a party of, say, six, this potato mound might measure some 8 inches long by 5 inches wide and 2 to 3 inches deep. This is nice also for a summer luncheon first course, or a Sunday supper, and would be popular at a schoolroom high tea.

All the vegetable purée soups made with milk and butter are nourishing and flesh-making. Here is an excellent one slightly different from the usual type; it was acquired during an enforced motor delay over suppertime at a small pension-farm on the Evian side of the Lake of Geneva.

POTAGE TAPIOCA MOUSSEUX.

Sprinkle into 1 pint veal stock about 2 dessertspoonfuls of fine tapioca such as Groults, and let it boil for 20 minutes. When ready to serve, slightly whip ¼ pint cream, pour it on to the soup, and whisk briskly till it all becomes frothy, serving it at once from a brown glazed soup tureen, well heated. Some milk and the yolk of an egg could be substituted for cream, but disadvantageously.

This American way of serving *Chicken à la Maryland* is good if the cook can devote some time and care to it, and it has been known to tempt a fugitive appetite.

Cut up a nice chicken in slices and joints, season with black pepper plentifully, and leave for 4 hours. Dip in a thin batter, and fry in butter till it is a golden colour; place it in a stewpan with a pint of cream, letting it simmer till the cream thickens. Serve with hominy (or maizena) cake made by boiling 1 pint milk with butter, pepper, salt, and 3 tablespoonfuls of the maizena. Slip in 1 whole egg and some grated parmesan cheese after the hominy or maizena is cooked. When cold, cut out in half-moon shaped pieces; egg, bread-crumb, and fry these; roast some bananas, skin and halve them across, and place round the chicken alternately with the fritters. Pour the cream sauce over the jointed pieces, and serve very hot.

Perhaps the most fattening of all savouries is a marrow bone on toast. But it is probably more popular with men than with women – as, indeed, are most varieties of boiled and toasted cheese, which, being mixed with butter, help to put on weight. An original form of savoury is *Bonne Bouche Otello*, made out of a couple of large French plums to each guest, or a single Carlsbad plum. They must be softened by soaking in a little hot water; one or two almonds, blanched and browned in melted butter and rolled in pepper, salt (and a little cayenne if liked hot) should be inserted in place of the extracted stone; roll in a thin rasher of bacon and grill on a skewer. Have ready *croûtes* of fried bread, slip out the skewer, lay the little plum grills on them, and serve very hot.

For those who prefer sweets to savouries, this recipe for a *Bombe Caramel* should be gratefully received, the formula being a family secret generously communicated.

Take 6 yolks of eggs and 2 whites, 1 tablespoonful castor sugar, and whisk them over boiling water until warm; withdraw and whip until cold, add a teacup of whipped cream, mix all together, put into a bombe mould, and freeze about 2 hours. When frozen scoop out centre, and fill with cold hard caramel made in the usual way and afterwards pounded and passed through a wire sieve. Sufficient for a pint mould for four persons. Serve with thin golden caramel sauce round and some crisp biscuits.

Lest these suggestions be considered too exacting in material or labour for some readers, a nice *Oatmeal Sunday Pudding* for family consumption is added.

Take 3 oz. coarse oatmeal, 3 oz. flour, 2 oz. butter (or margarine), 1½ oz. sugar, rind of 1 lemon, ½ teacupful treacle, ½ teaspoonful carbonate of soda, ½ teacupful milk, 2 oz. dried stoned and chopped raisins, ditto candied peel; rub butter into flour, add oatmeal, sugar, soda, fruit, rind, and bind together with warmed milk and treacle. Turn into a greased mould or basin; steam carefully for 2 or 3 hours. Turn out and serve with a sweet sauce or custard made hot.

The words inscribed on the Delphic Oracle, 'Know thyself' and 'Nothing too much', might well be written on our daily menu card, and in so far as they are observed will success and improvement accrue to the too thin.

For the Too Fat

We are reminded in Scripture that 'All flesh is grass,' but, as a great artist once added reassuringly, 'We cannot be sufficiently thankful that all grass is not flesh.' No one likes to be fat; it is unbecoming, fatiguing, and impairs efficiency. And although the condition is oftener the result of defective metabolism than of undue or indiscriminate appetite, still the experience of the war years, with their scarcity of the flesh-making foods, shows that weight *can* be reduced by a diminished consumption of dairy produce, sugar, and starchy foods. Unfortunately, all the nicer things are on a weights and measures black list, and the annual advice of an eminent financial authority to 'spend less' must be paraphrased into a diminished consumption of all nourishment for those who would grow thinner. The important drinking of sufficient fluid, moreover, should be transferred from meal times to a previous or subsequent hour. Such inconvenient advice is only acted on when it is given in return for payment by a medical expert, but there may possibly be some chance for a few gratuitous suggestions towards making an austere diet more varied and pleasurable than it often is.

LEMON TEA.

For the early morning luxury, substitute 2 freshly-cut, thin slices of lemon, on to which boiling water has been poured. This, sipped from a delicate china cup, is fragrant and thinning.

If that insidious enemy, soup, be held indispensable at dinner, at least avoid the vegetable purées and bisques made with cream, butter, root vegetables, and rich fish, also the savoury potage in which milk and flour figure, and try clear *Consommé à l'Estragon*, with its delicate and clean flavour.

Make the required quantity of clear vegetable stock in the usual way, or use a chicken carcass or some veal, if convenient, with ordinary stock. For garnish pick and blanch some 6d. worth of tarragon, letting half simmer gently for 30 minutes in the consommé. About 10 minutes before dinner, whisk the whites of 2 eggs stiffly with salt and pepper, adding the rest of the tarragon leaves, dried and finely chopped; take a heaped dessertspoonful of the whipped whites and drop each to the required number into a frying-pan of boiling water to poach for 3 minutes; pour the boiling soup into a hot tureen, drain each poached white, and let them float like snow islands on the top, serving one to each person.

Natural Meat Jelly is made by slow simmering of a little good beef, and is nourishing and palatable. Served very cold as jelly with a rusk, or re-heated with a couple of diet biscuits, it makes an adequate and sustaining little meal.

To give variety to plain roast or grilled meat, serve with it in a brown oven-proof dish some fresh *Rognons Sautés*, blanched, freed from fat and skin, and cut into thin slices; they only require cooking in stock thickened with a very little flour, and flavoured with wine, and mushroom, or tomato and chopped herbs. *Calves' Brains*, carefully washed and poached, can be served in the same sort of way from a white ramekin fireproof dish with a little *beurre noir* sauce mainly composed of diluted vinegar and lemon, a very little butter, and plenty of chopped parsley. This is good, too, with slightly devilled slices of lean meat. A *Salad à la Américaine*, made of the raw heart of a fresh young cabbage very finely shredded and diluted with some quite thin dressing made of raw yolks of eggs, and a little chili vinegar, served very cold, is a good accompaniment. Indeed, all green salads and many fruit ones may be used freely without risk of fattening, if dressed without rich sauce or abundant oil, lemon juice being substituted for vinegar for those of delicate digestion. A fresh or slightly pickled tongue is suitable food for those suffering from avoirdupois, though still somewhat expensive. This recipe for the humbler *Braised Sheep's Tongues, Sauce Piquante*, could also be adapted to the larger ox tongue.

Place cut-up carrot, onion, celery, leeks in a stewpan with a walnut of butter, and put in number of tongues required; fry gently, turning the tongues, and add 1 cupful good stock, 1 bay leaf, thyme, and parsley. Let all braise gently for 3 hours, adding more stock as it reduces. Take out the tongues, skin and trim them, reduce the stock to a glaze and pour it through a strainer over the tongues, dish up on a bed of spinach, and serve with sauce made by cutting up 1 small onion fine, reducing it in a stewpan with 2 tablespoonfuls of vinegar till nearly dry; then add 1 small cup brown stock, 1 walnut-sized piece of glaze, 1 teaspoonful Harvey sauce, and let all boil. Finally add a few blanched almonds and a small quantity of orange peel, both cut into fine strips, or 2 tablespoonfuls unsweetened stoned cherries. A larger quantity of cherries could be warmed in clear gravy and served round the larger tongue if preferred.

Mixed Grills are another stand-by for anti-fat meals and can be pleasantly varied. A small chicken jointed, spread with tamarind preserve and grilled with an accompaniment of mushrooms; mutton cutlets scored with chutney and grilled with tomato and chipolata saus-ages; game of all kinds slightly devilled and sent round with a dish of green watercress, stewed soft, drained, finely chopped, moistened with stock, reheated, and just before serving a little lemon juice stirred in with pepper and salt.

For a winter dessert, try a black plum or two from a two-pound glass screw jar, after the top layer has been extracted and some cherry brandy poured in, adding more as the liqueur is absorbed by the plums, and keep it air-tight for two or three weeks before use.

Activities, mental and physical, play a large part in reducing weight, just as sloth and inertia promote it, for, in the words of Claudel, 'Bien des choses se consument sur le feu d'un cœur qui brûle.'

Food for Travellers

The birds have not a monopoly of migration in our restless age. Every year winter sports, Riviera sunshine, Italian culture, or the lure of Monte Carlo summon the athletic, the invalid, the student, or the mere pleasure-seeker, in ever increasing numbers to pursue the insubstantial form of happiness to their chosen resorts.

Travellers in these times are reverting to the old-fashioned habit of taking their journey food with them, some actuated by motives of economy if the party be numerous, others by the discomforts of that dark and perilous pilgrimage from remote parts of a swaying train to the crowded restaurant car. Some have a preference for the food of their own choice, others would limit the opportunity of the hostile microbe. For prolonged journeys, then, with all their attendant uncertainties, it may be worth while to pack the fitted luncheon basket, and on it to superimpose a flat strapped overflow receptacle containing adequate provision of food and drink, if the way be long and the night cold. Most cooks lack both the imagination and experience necessary for such journey requirements, and have thereby brought the home-packed hamper into disrepute; but there is no reason why ham sandwiches and desiccated seed-cake should be the sole and inevitable refreshments provided.

Attractive presentation of travellers' fare has a large

share in its success. Many of the big Stores, particularly those with American connections, specialize in the provision of papier-maché plates, dishes, and jars, of collapsible cups, and paper napkins. The food should be daintily packed in greaseproof paper with an outer wrapping of foolscap tied with fine twine and the contents marked outside. A nest of horn or aluminium drinking cups, together with a washable roll of American cloth or silver aeroplane waterproof to hold cheap knives, forks, and spoons, can easily be provided if the basket be not a fully fitted one. For the food itself here are some suggestions, which must be dependent on individual tastes, on the length of the journey, on the purse of the traveller. Hard-boiled eggs accompanied by green sandwiches of lettuce or watercress, a small wisp of oriental salt, or Cerebos, mixed with coarsely-ground black pepper for each traveller, are always a good stand-by; the breasts of chickens or pheasants, partridges or grouse, enriched perhaps with a little purée of foie gras or thin coating of savoury aspic; a salad of cold potato and lettuce, sparingly moistened with thin mayonnaise in a grease-paper-lined cardboard dish, can be the *pièce de résistance*. Packets of sandwiches can be multiplied according to numbers and need, and varied indefinitely, for, good as those of nicely-made ham, tongue, or pressed beef can be, they have that familiarity which often breeds indifference, and it is wonderful what can be done to invest them with surprised interest by a touch of chutney, or Cumberland sauce, of tarragon flavoured vinegar on their green salad addition, of a slice of beetroot powdered with chopped gherkin, or of tomato sprinkled with capers. Sandwiches of foie gras of well-known brands are for the rich, but this humbler counterfeit can be recommended.

HOME-MADE FOIE GRAS.

One pound of chicken livers or 2 goose livers, about ¼ lb. fat bacon. Cut the bacon into small pieces, put into a frying-pan and fry it slowly, then add the livers cut up small, and sprig of thyme and bay leaf. Add a tablespoonful of brandy or sherry and fry altogether about 10 minutes, then put into the mortar and pound well, removing herbs; pass through a fine wire sieve, then mix up with a little cream, salt, and pepper. Put into a pot, pressing all well together, and pour over a little clarified butter to keep out the air. Small pieces of truffle are a great addition to the flavour, and should be added with the cream.

Sandwiches of thinnest gruyère between biscuits, or bread spread with green butter are excellent, and this is easily made and welcome in winter and summer, giving variety to the cheese course.

SAVOURY GREEN BUTTER.

A ¼ lb. good fresh butter. A couple of handfuls of spinach, boiled, drained, and passed through a hair sieve, the pulp obtained saved in a bowl. Bone and wipe off the oil of 6 anchovies, pass through sieve and save pulp. Mince finely a tablespoonful of curled parsley, ditto a teaspoonful of capers. Colour the butter first by working in the spinach greening, then add the other ingredients and turn into a block or an attractive small mould, or use for sandwiches after hardening in the ice box. The inventive cook will vary her butter by using sardines, lobster, prawns, crab meat, and flavouring with cress, gherkins, olives, etc., and colouring red with lobster coral, or mixing with crab.

Sandwiches of fruit for the children are popular. Round slices of banana sprinkled with orange juice and white centrifugal sugar, or of thinly-cut apple with grated walnuts, sandwiches of cream cheese with a thin spread of red currant jelly, of egg with sardine or anchovy, of celery shredded and creamed and sprinkled with plentiful yolk of hard-boiled egg, sandwiches of sponge-cake spread with chocolate or coffee icing, sandwiches of pastry with jam or glazed with thin caramel. Here is a recipe for lemon cheese cake mixture to fill light puff paste tartlets, for though a familiar dish it admits of as many classes as the Tripos, and this should be in Class I.

LEMON CHEESE CAKE MIXTURE.

Two large lemons, 3 oz. butter, ½ lb. lump sugar, 3 eggs. Put butter in the saucepan first, then add the juice and grated rind of lemons, then beat up eggs and stir them in, continue stirring till it thickens, put into very light puff pastry tartlets, and only use quite fresh.

The platform café au lait, so dear to the memory of generations of travellers, should not be missed when available, for the dread experience of the crossing is behind, and the joys of a sunshine holiday await us; but in case the 'dix minutes d'arrêt' prove but an insubstantial dream, this *Chelsea Bun* should be included in the basket, for it will be welcome alike in the cold dawn with a thermos of hot coffee, or with the etna and tea basket to enliven the long afternoon.

CHELSEA BUN.

Half a pound flour, 5 oz. butter or margarine, 1 oz. sugar, pinch of salt, 3 eggs, ½ oz. yeast. Mix the yeast with 2 oz. of the flour and a little tepid milk to make a light dough, place it to rise about 10 minutes. With the rest of the flour, put in sugar, eggs, and salt; beat well together, then mix in melted butter; then add the yeast, and work well together and stand in a cool place overnight. In the morning add the grated rind of a lemon or 2 small ones, a few sultanas, and some chopped peel. Form into a round on a baking sheet with a band of greased paper, brush over with egg, and stand in a warm place to rise a little. Place in not too hot an oven, and bake for about ½ hour.

A lemon or two slipped in for Chinese Russian tea, together with a tin of peptonized cocoa and milk, a tin of best consommé capsules, some dried milk powder easily mixed with water, a slab of first-rate chocolate – these will provide hot drinks in variety. Mineral waters and light wines are readily procurable by the way, if space has forbidden their inclusion at home. No experienced traveller starts without a flask of brandy, and the relative merits of biscuits (a matter of personal preferences) are too well known to need recalling. Fruit is of all forms of refreshment the most wholesome and welcome on a journey, and the dried forms – almonds and raisins, dates, and the crystallized varieties – are excellent and portable.

The travellers' food basket, equipped in some such ways as are here suggested, will render its owners independent of time and place, fortified against hunger and thirst, immune to the extortions and insolence of officials, and they will be fresh and ready on arrival to enjoy the lovely sights and gay adventures awaiting them, for has it not been truly said: 'We need all our sense to be aware of spirit'?

Food for Artists and Speakers

Musical and dramatic artists as well as public speakers and lecturers find that they cannot give out their best very soon after a substantial meal. When their effort is over, they are often either nervously exhausted and disinclined to eat – in which case they require nourishing but easily-digested and tempting food; or else they are so hungry that they eat freely of anything available, with resultant indigestion and restlessness, just when they most urgently require calm and refreshing sleep before another public appearance. Those who have sown unto us spiritual things have a claim on the harvest of our worldly things; for, unless well cared for materially, they can neither raise mortals to the skies, nor yet call angels down. Parliamentary elections, too, have horrid possibilities of recurrence, with their nightmare train of exhausting effort and disordered home-life; and a little care in the selection and preparation of suitable foods may even turn the tide of fortune, and enable politicians to scorn fatigue or illness and lead on to victory.

A slight supplement to a late 5 o'clock tea is the usual practice for those with a public appearance before them, and eggs, boiled, poached, or *en cocotte*, with savoury sandwiches are the most obvious addition to the tea-table. A small white china ramekin case filled with this quickly-made *Mousse of Egg and Sardine*, to be spread on thin crisp toast, is often useful, and within the compass of the humblest cook. Take a hard-boiled egg and pass it through a sieve into a basin; skin and bone four small sardines and pass through a sieve. Mix these two with a filbert-sized piece of fresh butter; add pepper, and moisten all with a little cream if available. Good also for breakfast as a change from marmalade.

Mrs. Gladstone's practice of sending her husband into battle on an egg-flip, cleverly produced at the psychological moment, can be imitated with this *Frothed Wine Soup*, good for a prima donna or pianist soon going into action, and can be made by anybody who can whisk an egg.

Beat 3 yolks of quite fresh eggs to a froth with a whisk over the fire, adding a small teaspoonful each of fine flour and white sugar, half a bottle of white wine, and half that quantity of water. Whisk till it comes to the boil, then take it off and serve immediately before the froth subsides. This quantity amply suffices for two.

At a Paris restaurant much frequented by the stars of the Comédie Française, these *Œufs Pochés en Surprise* were recently *the* popular 'plat,' of which the chef obligingly communicated the recipe to an artist patron.

Carefully poach as many new-laid eggs as required. When done, slip them into a basin of cold water; allow 2 thin slices from a good ham for each egg. Place the drained and trimmed egg on a slice of ham, putting another slice on top, repeating this for each egg. Lay them delicately in a long dish, sufficiently deep for their covering over in some aspic jelly, not very stiff, and delicately flavoured with tarragon. When set, cut them out with an oval tin cutter, and with a fish-slice place them on a silver dish, garnish with green salad, and serve with bread and butter sandwiches. They appear like midget galantines of savoury jelly, concealing the softly cooked egg hidden inside, and are both light and nourishing.

For those requiring more solid food, and yet unable to face suppers such as mixed grills, or sausages and mashed potatoes with lager beer, here are two recipes which might also be useful for other occasions.

SOLES AU GRATIN.

Butter a long fireproof dish; fillet some fair-sized soles; chop 2 large mushrooms, a piece of fat bacon the size of a walnut, a sprig of thyme and parsley, and a shalot very fine; mix with 2 handfuls of fine bread-crumbs, pepper and salt, and the juice of ½ lemon. Spread a layer of the mixture at the bottom of the dish, on it place the fillets of soles, cover with the remainder, place in a moderate oven for about 30 minutes, and just before serving pour a glass of white wine over, and serve in the same dish.

POULET À LA CRÊME.

Cut 1 or 2 small tender chickens in half, rub them with salt and papprika pepper. Put a good lump of butter in small pieces into a stewpan with some thin slices of streaky bacon. Cover these with a layer of onions cut into thin rings and put the pan on the fire. When the contents begin to smoke, add the half chickens, and let them stew on a slow fire for 1½ hour, when they should be a light brown. Remove from pan, carve into pieces and lay on a hot dish. Replace stewpan on fire, and add ½ pint sour cream, stirring constantly with a wooden spoon. Pour this sauce upon the chickens, and serve very hot; on no account add water or stock to this sauce.

Tartines Tricolor made a popular supper delicacy at a house beloved by musicians and actors in pre-war days.

Take thin round slices 2½ to 3 inches across from a long French roll or fresh loaf, butter sparingly, and lay slantingly across these open rounds thin strips alternately of white chicken (or turkey), of red tongue (or ham), of pickled cucumber (or mildly salted gherkin), varied by a thin fillet of anchovy washed in milk if too salt, and dish these flat with a light sprinkling of small cress in the centre.

An alternative might be the small oblong crisp toast sandwiches popular at West End bridge clubs, with a tiny roll, little finger size, of crisply fried streaky bacon, served in covered muffin dishes piping hot, and welcome on a chilly night.

On hot evenings the spent artist might dream, like the Sick King in Bokhara, 'of cherries served in drifts of snow', but muscat grapes, skinned and pipped, reposing in a pond of delicious calvesfoot lemon jelly in a flat glass dish, would be more wholesome and nourishing. Or when muscats are out of season, try this reviving

GELÉE À LA BOURGOGNE.

Half a bottle of fairly good claret, 3 oz. white sugar, half a sherry glass of brandy, the thin rind and juice of one good lemon, ½ teacup raspberry jam or jelly, boiled together with 4 or 5 leaves of gelatine according to temperature, or ½ oz. of isinglass. Strain through a muslin, and set in a mould with a hollow centre for the reception of sweetened whipped cream. In hot weather use ice for stiffening jelly and cream.

These should all prove good preludes to 'Great Nature's second course, chief nourisher in life's great feast'.

Food for the Punctual
and the Unpunctual

In a delightful chapter in Plutarch's *Lives* describing the home life of Antony, Lampryas tells of his visit to the kitchen, where he saw 'a world of diversities of meats, amongst them eight wild boars roasting whole, and wonderful sumptuous preparations for one supper'. When he inquired as to the number of guests expected the cook fell a-laughing and said: 'Not above twelve in all, yet all must be served in whole or it might be marred, for Antoninus peradventure will sup presently, or it may be a pretty while hence, or likely enough he will defer it long, for he hath drunken well to-day, or he may have some great matters in hand; and therefore we do not dress *one* supper only, but *many* suppers, because we are uncertain of the hour he will sup in.'

He is a bold man who would call on his cook for such devotion and elasticity in these days!

In unjust contrast this passage from Hawkesworth's Life of Dr. Swift shows what can befall a punctual and deserving master: 'The dean had a kitchen wench for his cook, a woman of a large size, robust constitution and coarse features, her face very much seamed with the smallpox and furrowed by age; this woman he always distinguished by the name "Sweetheart". It happened one day that "Sweetheart" greatly over-roasted the only joint he had for dinner; upon which he sent for her, and with great coolness and gravity: "Sweetheart," says he, "take this down into the kitchen and do it less." She replied that was impossible. "Pray, then," said he, "if you had roasted it too little, could you have done it more?" "Yes," she said, easily could she have done that. "Why, then, Sweetheart," replied the dean, "let me advise you, if you must commit a fault, commit a fault that can be mended." '

The punctual and the unpunctual are always with us, so it is a wise cook who knows her own master, and in preparing dinner she may like to make choice of these few suggestions according to the measure of her hope or her experience.

For the Punctual:

POULET GRILLÉ SAINT JEAN.

Bone a nice chicken, or, if a novice, let it be boned at the purveyor for future imitation. Prepare a farce from veal or the best parts of a rabbit in the usual way, with ½ teacupful cream, 1 whole egg, and seasoning added to the pounded meat. Fill the inside of the boned bird, which will be spread out flat, with the farce, and cook under the gas or electric griller. Serve it, preferably, on a silver-plated grill above a meat dish, or on a long fire-proof dish, cut right across in thick 1 inch slices, with perfectly-made bread-sauce, gravy, and a garnish of watercress, or a cold Tartar sauce if preferred.

SOUFFLÉ DE PRUNES À LA RUSSE.

Boil ½ lb. French plums till soft, rub through a hair sieve, keep the purée soft and moist; whisk into it by degrees whilst hot 6 whites of eggs. Fill the mixture into a low plated dish and bake for 10 minutes in a sharp oven. Send up with some vanilla iced cream served separately, or some small blobs of stiffly-whipped cream dropped on the top of the soufflé as it goes in.

For the Unpunctual, try a savoury dish of *Papprika*, thus: –

Skin 4 large onions, cut up, and stew them a bright golden colour with 6 oz. fresh butter. Rub this through a fine sieve with ½ pint sour cream, a saltspoonful of salt, ½ teaspoonful Papprika pepper (procurable at all Stores), and add your previously jointed and cooked chicken, or slices of cooked meat, game, or rabbit; let this heat thoroughly and slowly; serve in a casserole with plain boiled rice, slightly flavoured with Papprika, and a green vegetable.

ICED CHICKEN SOUFFLÉ WITH CURRIED LIVERS.

Pound the breast of a boiled chicken, adding ½ pint béchamel sauce, and pass it through a hair sieve. Whip ½ pint cream; add it to the chicken. Take a white fireproof soufflé dish, stand a small jar in the centre, filling the soufflé dish around with the chicken cream. Set it in the ice cave for some 2 hours. Remove jar and fill in the space with 6 or 8 curried chicken livers, trimmed, and put in a stewpan with a walnut of butter, and seasoning. Cook these for some 10 minutes; add 1 teaspoonful each of curry powder, curry paste, and 1 tablespoonful desiccated cocoanut (previously steeped and stirred in hot milk and most of the nut part eliminated) and a little chopped shallot. Let the livers cook in this for another 10 minutes to absorb most of the moisture before letting them get cold and adding to the chicken soufflé. With this serve cold curried rice and brown bread-and-butter sandwiches with a little chutney in them.

For a long-suffering sweet, try this *Apricot Purée*.

Stew 1 lb. best evaporated apricots after an all-night soak. When cooked soft, add a small tin of peeled apricots; boil together, sweetening to taste; reduce the syrup, pass through a wire sieve, and put into a shallow glass bowl; cover completely with a thin layer of partly-whipped cream (about 6d. worth), and perhaps a few chopped pistachio nuts to embellish. With this send round a glass finger-bowl of that useful American cereal 'puffed rice' just crisped in the oven, to be sprinkled on by each guest. This sweet is suitable also for holiday luncheons or Sunday suppers.

'It is better to be punctual than to be sorry,' is an admonition that has often embarrassed apologetic youth; but fortunately women are by nature forgiving, and the erring often more lovable than the faultless.

Home Thoughts of Florence
and Some Tuscan Recipes

To tax and to please, like to love and to be wise, is not given to man, wrote Burke, that incomparable artist in the concise expression of great truths, and those who have suffered under the burdens of taxation since the Great War, and experienced the increasing difficulty of adjusting income to expenditure, are apt to think that life is less difficult in the sunny south than under grey English skies. To impoverished poets, artists, and writers, to all those with more past than present, Florence has ever offered the treasures of her beauty, of her sunshine and flowers, at moderate cost and with generous hands; and though ninepence for fourpence is not really easier to find there than at home, it may often take the hopeful wanderer some time to discover this truth. Two such wanderers, having come thus far, decided that it was useless to indulge in vain regrets, for 'the gods were right when they forbade Orpheus to look behind.' Better far to enjoy the delights proffered so freely on all sides, and to forget for a while, if possible, the sordid limitations of a reduced income.

One of the economists varied her Mornings in Florence at the shrines of Giotto and Fra Angelico, of Botticelli and Michael Angelo, with others spent in a delightful '*cucinetta*' under the guidance of a smiling adept, who revealed the mysteries of Pasti and Legumi, of Minestrone and Frittura, of Insalata and Dolce, with obliging charm.

There is no hunger like that engendered in picture galleries, no fatigue comparable to that of the conscientious sightseer after prolonged contemplation of the world's masterpieces. Let us recapture, if may be, some of those simple Tuscan dishes offered to exhausted culture in exile, but equally enjoyable whether there or here.

First let us, like the cheerful windmills bickering across the valleys in R. L. Stevenson's earliest journey to the Lowlands, engage ourselves 'in the happy occupation of making bread'. Not that bitter bread of exile known to the poet, but that agreeable form called *Panettone*, so greatly enjoyed by Mr. and Mrs. Robert Browning at sunny breakfasts in Casa Guidi. And if you wish to be truly Florentine, you will also learn to make, and like, *Gressini*, which can keep a hungry man nibbling patiently whilst the *Polenta* or the *Risotto* of his choice takes on the finishing touches preparatory to its savoury advent, heralded by the encouraging prelude: 'Restono serviti, Signori, buon pranzo!'

PANETTONE.

One pound of flour, ½ lb. butter or less, ¼ lb. sugar, ¼ lb. raisins, 3 eggs, lemon peel grated, ½ oz. of baker's yeast. Mix flour overnight with a little water and some baker's yeast in a basin with 1 egg and a little butter to form a not very stiff paste. Cover with a cloth and stand in a warm place all night to rise. In the morning, when it should have risen well, add remaining butter, dissolve the 2 eggs, sugar, peel, and raisins. Mix to medium consistency, and make this into a round roughly moulded flat loaf. If the dough is not stiff enough to keep in shape confine within a metal ring some 9 inches across, and bake until it has doubled its size in a moderate oven. Then make a large cross on it, brush with white of egg, sprinkle with pounded sugar and scraps of butter, and finish in a quick oven.

GRESSINI.

Half a pound of flour and pinch of salt, ½ oz. butter, saltspoonful baking powder. Put these in a basin and mix with boiling water, not very moist. Then turn out and knead well until quite smooth, and roll with hands into sticks about the thickness of a cedar pencil, and some 9 or 10 inches long. Bake in a moderate oven till quite hard throughout, which takes a long time. They should be crisp and biscuit-coloured, and are served in dozens, with bread, in baskets abroad.

POLENTA AU GRATIN.

Into a pint of boiling water (salted) pour about a breakfast cup of polenta, or maize flour, stir well, boil for 25 minutes, add 2 oz. butter and some 2 oz. of parmesan cheese. Spread this on a buttered baking sheet. When cold cut into rounds the size of a wine glass; brown the rounds of polenta in butter each side in a frying-pan, lay them just overlapping in a buttered fireproof dish, with grated parmesan and nut-brown butter poured over, and finish in the oven. Serve very hot. If preferred, a creamy cheesy sauce can be poured over the polenta rounds and put into the oven to brown.

RISOTTO.

Put into a stewpan 1 pint good stock, preferably veal, ¼ lb. rice (Italian the best). Cook slowly with a pinch of saffron tied in muslin, to be removed when rice is cooked. Take a small onion cut into dice and fry in butter, also a couple of skinned tomatoes, or some mushrooms cut in slices and fried, and ¼ lb. grated parmesan. Add all these to the rice with a walnut-sized piece of butter, stirring all carefully together, and salt to taste. If too stiff add a little more stock. Scraps of white chicken cut in shreds, or their livers fried in butter, can be placed on the top of the risotto. The Milanese add beef marrow and white wine; the Neapolitans season with pounded prawns and garnish with lobster. Fragments of pork or of truffles can be brought to the service of this dish, whose infinite variety need never stale with custom.

MONT BLANC.

Italians are fond of sweets, but unimaginative in their preparation. Here is a delicious one, for which the chestnuts of Vallombrosa yearly patter to the ground in their thousands. Take of them, roasted and peeled, 1 lb., and put in a stewpan with vanilla pod, ¼ lb. sugar, a little milk, ¼ lb. of best chocolate. Cook till soft. Rub through coarse sieve into a basin-shaped mould well sprinkled with grated chocolate. Turn out, and mask to whiteness with thinly whipped sweetened cream. Serve cold on a silver dish.

Of Good Taste in Food

No double meaning lurks in this heading, but it is not recognized perhaps as generally as it might be that the selection, preparation, and service of food have their own codes of fitness and quality, their rules governing cause and result, which cannot be ignored or transgressed without detriment to all concerned. Too much effort given to material things entails neglect of spiritual ones, too little induces loss of temper, money, and health. Some rare spirits there are who may discipline themselves into indifference to creature comforts, who may write magical poetry on lumpy porridge, paint glorious pictures on indifferent eggs, lead armies to victory on bully beef – we salute them and pass on! But with those who, whilst lifting reverential eyes to the stars, yet know and love this kind, warm earth, we would take counsel awhile. It is not thought praiseworthy to wear nasty clothes, to have ugly flowers in the garden, dull books on the table, comfortless furniture in the home, and horrid pictures on the walls. Why, then, are God's good gifts of food and drink to be spoiled by stupidity and mismanagement? The French are artists in these matters, and yet of France it is said –

A country that can think, and, thinking, acts;
A country that can act, and, acting, dreams –

Let us not, then, be too highbrow to learn something both theoretically and practically about food and cookery, or too lazy to take trouble anew every morning; neither let us be so timorous as to sit down under a rule of what a schoolboy friend in a recent examination paper alluded to as 'that practice introduced by the Greeks of a man having only one wife which is called *Monotony*.'

The dishes which will befit a king's banquet or a Lord Mayor's feast look strange and out of place in modest surroundings. Turtle soup, plum-pudding, and champagne for an August Sunday luncheon in a seaside villa would be, to say the least, incongruous, but have been experienced.

A blue-blooded and conservative marquis may be forgiven his temporary loss of self-control when the newly-engaged cook sent on its gay career round a decorous dinner-party of county neighbours a transparent and highly decorated pink ice pudding concealing within inmost recesses a fairy light and a musical box playing the 'Battle of Prague.' Words were spoken, and, like the chord of self in Locksley Hall, this over-elaborated creation 'passed in music out of sight.'

Matters of taste must be felt, not dogmatized about. A large cray-fish or lobster rearing itself menacingly on its tail seems quite at home on the sideboard of a Brighton hotel-de-luxe, but will intimidate a shy guest at a small dinner-party. A story quoted by Sydney Smith from an old chronicle records a dinner prepared for a meeting of bishops at Dort, one of the dishes being 'a roasted peacock, having in lieu of tail the arms and banners of the Archbishop, which was a goodly sight to such as favour the Church.' What a contrast to the practices prevailing in even the more stately homes of the Anglican clergy! A great prelate of our own day is said to be contemplating drastic changes in a home life rendered difficult by the limitations of his cook, whose only alternative to a burnt offering, as he complained, was a bleeding sacrifice.

Over-elaboration then, even in our kindest cooks, must be discouraged: games of dominoes played in truffles over the chicken cream, birds' nests counterfeited round the poached eggs, jazzing jellies, and castellated cakes show misdirection of energy. Not that an occasional exception may not prove the rule – let it be made on behalf of *Gelée Crème de Menthe*, an emerald-green pool, set in a flat glass bowl, reminiscent of Sabrina fair in her home below translucent waves, or of Capri caverns, cool and deep; whilst the delicate aroma of peppermint will recall to Presbyterian minds those Sabbath indulgences practised by young and old at kirk in far-off Highland glens.

Make a quart of good lemon jelly in the approved way, preferably with calves' feet, more probably with best leaf gelatine, but not – oh! not – with jelly powders. Whilst warm add a handful of those large green peppermint geranium leaves, thick as a fairy's blanket, soft as a vicuna robe, and to be found in most old-fashioned gardens, and let them flavour your blend; or you can use 3 or 4 drops of essence of peppermint, ½ teaspoonful of apple green to colour, or home-made spinach greening for a substitute. Pass through your jelly bag and serve very cold. A glass of crème de menthe might well improve this, but is by no means indispensable.

To mollify the fastidious purist or placate the pepper-mint hater, prelude this recipe with an excellent *Consommé Fausse Tortue*. Elderly aldermen will bless you for it, and the hunters home from the hill will forget the rigours of the chase, and be warmed and comforted.

Having removed the brains from half a calf's head, put it in a stewpan with a little salt and water to cover, and bring it to the boil, then place it under cold water tap and thoroughly wash. Put it back into the clean stewpan with enough stock or stock water to cover it, plenty of stock vegetables, also bay leaf, and a few allspice. Simmer gently for 5 hours, then strain, and leave to set. Next day remove fat, and clarify, adding a turtle tablet and some turtle soup herbs as sold at Stores. When clear, strain through a clean cloth, re-boil, add a little sherry, salt, pepper, to taste, and, just before serving, some pieces of the meat cut in gelatinous squares from the head and indistinguishable from green fat, two for each portion, of which there might be eight.

This would be a propitious moment for asking some favour, dropping out casually a regrettable piece of news, or even confessing to the near advent of an unwelcome visitor. It is wonderful how safely awkward corners can be turned and dangerous seas navigated without disaster if only the tactful moment be chosen for the venture.

GREAT  FOOD

THROUGHOUT the history of civilization, food has been livelihood, status symbol, entertainment – and passion. The twenty fine food writers here, reflecting on different cuisines from across the centuries and around the globe, have influenced each other and continue to influence us today, opening the door to the wonders of every kitchen.